A Companion for Owls

A Companion for Owls

Being the Commonplace Book

of D. Boone, Long Hunter,

Back Woodsman, &c.

MAURICE MANNING

Harcourt, Inc.

Orlando   Austin   New York   San Diego   Toronto   London

www.HarcourtBooks.com

Library of Congress Cataloging-in-Publication Data
Manning, Maurice, 1966–
A companion for owls: being the commonplace book of D. Boone,
long hunter, back woodsman, &c./Maurice Manning.
p.   cm.
Includes bibliographical references.
ISBN 0-15-101049-8
1. Boone, Daniel, 1734–1820—Poetry.   2. Frontier and pioneer life—Poetry.
3. Explorers—Poetry.   4. Pioneers—Poetry.   5. Kentucky—Poetry.
6. Hunters—Poetry.   I. Title.
PS3613.A5654C66 2004
811'.6—dc22   2004002768

Text set in Van Dijck
Designed by Cathy Riggs

Printed in the United States of America

First edition
K J I H G F E D C B A

This book is dedicated to my father,

ATWM, True Son of Pioneers,

and to the memory of DBM, the Great Scout.

Daniel Boone was born November 2, 1734, near present-day Reading, Pennsylvania. He was a skilled hunter and was knowledgeable in all manner of woodcraft. He helped establish the earliest settlements in Kentucky, the fifteenth state, and the first state that had not been under British colonial authority. Boone had many adventures during his long life. He died in Missouri on September 26, 1820.

CONTENTS

Meditations

Fancies

Letters From Squire

Apologies

Illustrations, Inventories, and Maps

Histories, lives, portraits, characters! What are all those? Ingenious novels constructed upon a few external actions, upon a few speeches that relate to them, on some subtle conjectures in which the Author seeks much more to shine than to find out the truth.

—*The Confessions of Jean-Jacques Rousseau*

Meditations

The moral sense, or conscience, is as much a part of man, as his leg or arm. It is given to all human beings in a stronger or weaker degree, as force of members is given them in a greater or less degree. It may be strengthened by exercise, as may any particular limb of the body. This sense is submitted indeed in some degree, to the guidance of reason; but it is a small stock which is required for this: even a less one than what we call Common sense. State a moral case to a ploughman and a professor. The former will decide it as well, and often better than the latter, because he has not been led astray by artificial rules.

—Thomas Jefferson, letter to Peter Carr, 1787

On God

Is there a god of the gulf between a man
and a horse? A god who hovers above the trench
of difference? Not a god who makes us notice;
but a god who rakes his hand through the air and makes
a space neither can enter. What about
a god of animal innards? Some god
whose sole creation cleans the blood of an elk?
Perhaps there's a god of petty disaster
who breaks wagon wheels and paints clouds across
an old man's eyes. Consider the gods of flint
and primer who work side by side with the gods
of spark and steel; then there's the god of aim
and the god of near death—a god commonly praised.
Consider a god of small spaces, a fat
man's misery god, who lives in the shadow
between two rocks and sleeps on moss, content
with the smallness of his task; the god who bends
rivers, the god who flecks the breast of a hawk,
the god who plunders saltworks. I once thought
one god looked over my shoulder and measured
my steps, but now I believe that god is outnumbered
and I am surrounded by countless naked gods,
like spores or dust or birds or trees on fire,
the song, the grit, the mean seed of nakedness.

First

Arriving, we walked down as if we were hill-born
and bred to know only hills, so that the end of hills
was surprising, rolling out before us like a woman's
skirts gathered and fanned across her lap, like loosely
folded fabric, like calico: spotted and patchworked
as if some big-fingered god had gently smudged
the world he made. Our horses and our dogs paused.
We had not expected glory and it stopped us dead,
which is not altogether uncommon: Moses spying
Canaan, for example, must have first stood silent
before waving his people ahead, the land smothered
in half shadow, half-light like velvet, and steadied
himself, one hand firm on his staff, the other reaching
to his brow, wiping his gray hair back. So I walked
into Kentucky barefooted and clumsy as if I had
sneaked out of school to cheat my lessons and come
upon a girl waiting for me behind a beech tree,
wondering where on earth I'd been. I stood still
on the invisible line and spit across it onto the new
map, making my first mark, wondering if I could
keep such a dark and bloody secret to myself.

Without a Vision

I saw all Israel scattered on the mountains...(1 Kings 22:17)

Don't ever name a son Israel;
and don't ever follow a man hot
for blood into battle, because
he will bring blood upon you:
that is the one wage of vengeance.
If a man named McGary declares
you yellow, pretend you're deaf;
don't ride behind him to a place
called the Blue Licks. That way,
if you do have a son named Israel,
you will never have to watch him
fall and find him five days later,
buzzards maddened at his throat,
their wings tipped with his blood,
his body torn in sundry pieces,
like a wandering nation, dispersed.
You cannot bury such a vision; Israel
keeps returning to me in wavering
remnants, which is troubling, because
I come from a generation which knows
very little about irony; and now history
will look back and wonder what on earth
I was thinking, whatever led me to follow.
Sometimes, it is a high price we pay for blinking;
you question that a nation could depend on one
man, and then, in a moment, you realize it does.

The Meaning of Time

On occasion I would meet an Indian
in possession of a broken pocket watch
(one no doubt bartered from the British or
plundered from a dead settler), who had
no idea he held a device to measure minutes
and hours, who had no notion of gears
and had a one-sided concept of springs:
simple objects of flow, mouths spilling out
the watery secrets of the netherworld.
Would such an Indian study the frozen
hands and face to see how long it takes
to make a fire, gut a buffalo? Is sunlight
dripping on the leaves a question suitable
for clocks? Can a wounded man be spoken
of in terms of neutral hours? Is the whole
world endlessness? Yes, it is. The world
is endless cause and need, slow motion
and design. The world is irreversible,
no matter how much you let it tick down:
a white man boiling berries, tying and retying
his purse strings; a red man staring at the sky;
a silver case flashing moonlight: there is no
measure or meaning in this low world:
the present is always passing away; what matters
is nature, with even-tempered mischief, always
breaking her own rules, like a child at play.

The Sum Result of Speculation

Three long-legged paces is a rod on flat
ground; four is a Kentucky rod. One acre
is one hundred sixty square rods. Marking
off thousand-acre parcels is a lot of paces,
a lot of steps to count in your head,
especially if you have a bad tooth tolling
every step you take. Sometimes I would
take thirty-five paces in one direction,
then forty in another and say I had an acre;
sometimes I zigzagged through this rolling
country and guessed. One time I dug
a rotten tooth out of my jaw with a rifle flint
so I wouldn't lose count. One hundred twelve
paces is a mile. Two thousand acres is three
square miles. I don't know how many
lonely paces my feet have trod. I don't know
how many trees I've marked with numbers,
or how often I've been generous, or if
I should be faulted. I'm sad to say,
walking this country for money only
brought me loss; but I never once got lost.

A Possible Blessing

It's good to see the world as dying out—
an ember in an ashpit, a locust husk
still clinging to an elder bough, a stone
turned up by a silvered plow, or a man who smears
his face against his sleeve, as if he wants
to wipe away his name and leave a blank.

The sense of last is like the sense of first
and one is almost the same as nothing; yet,
some joy is part of fading, part of being
culled for one purpose which is rightly called,
unapologetic loss: you are the sun
of an insignificant world, a kiss
blown off a cliff, true love without the chance
to be denied—the unrequited life!

Frozen to its shell is the locust's jagged smile;
the stone chuckles back into the earth;
the coal extinguishes itself and gloats;
the man who understands diminishment
will lay down in his coffin from time to time
and practice disappearing, like a bug
riding a twig on a stream: a speck of un-
belonging, immersed in careless undulation.
You lose your obligation to remember,
which frees you to the quickened world of matter.

Is grace forgetting we are but specks
in the iris of a monstrous eye?

Eight Analytical Questions

Who decides the shape of rocks,
the curl of cedar branches, the ripples
wrinkled down a bedrock stream?
Why do I dream of crows winking like black eyes across the sky?
Who discovered salt? What is the source of two objects
against each other: a bug against a leaf,
the leaf against a bed of moss, the moss
against the earth, the earth against the womb
the moon has made from circling the earth, the womb
against the boundless sea of heaven? Who
decreed when spring should start? Whose task is it
to grant the rain permission to fall and feed
the rivers? Who draws rings around the hearts of trees?
Upon my soul, I wonder who invented beauty?

Dog Day

The way one foot falls soft, not from stalking game,
but merely stepping into a meadow, I
pronounce myself, lord of no manor house,
the lord of nothing, but one bad ankle bone,
which is enough dominion for me. This place,
the haunt of buffalo and elk: I wear
their skins; the grasses smooth beneath my feet.
My gun is sleeping in a hollow log
and I am harmless in this world. What need
has Man for treaties? What depends on forts?
No truce and no provision can erase
the children I have buried, the slaughter I
have made. My horse is tethered to a tree;
my pouch is full of ginseng root: I leave
it in a fairy ring. My clothes I bury.
Before this place I am a naked feist.

That I Am Essential to Creation

Each day divides itself,
measure for measure's sake.

Time's hinge is oiled by such
trifles, a gasp, a gape,
broken in two like bread—
over and overness—
needed or not they come,
vision and sound one loaf;
even the crumbs will count.

Crawling across my face,
crickets deny my form:
shadow instead of man,
dark and unleavened space.

Woolly worms warm to me,
thinking I am a tree
fallen on their behalf.

Beauty insists itself.

Cold now, I smell the fall
waiting with bated breath.

Season of summary,
vessel and yoke of sleep,
make me your spit and clay:
hollow should be my name.

Schuylkill Country, 1742

I was playing Bye Baby Bunting with three
of my backwoods Delaware friends; we had
a rabbit skin and maple switches, we
were naked to the waist; my mother had
her bucket and she called me to her side:

I swanny but I believe I've borned a red'un—
I have a legend for your little ears
if ye will help me milk these ornery cows.

As I was always keen for yarns, I complied.
We tied two nervous cusses to a tree;
she asked had I heard tell of the Madog man...
When we were done, I unhitched the cows and turned
them out. My mother laid a finger on my brow:

You must live your life, my child, but live it by
the light that burns in thine own heart, even
if it's red. She laughed and added just this verse:

Madoc wismio ydie wedd
Jawn yenan Owen Gwynedd
Ni sennum dir sy enriddoedd
Ni do mawr ondy moroedd.

What else could better set a young boy's heart
afire, what else could turn his blue eyes wild?

On the Whole, the World Is Level

Possessed of chigger bites and fleas,
a man must stop his travels and scratch
from time to time. He brews a paste
of herbs and tallow and smoothes it on
his skin. His ankles, knees, and armpits
resemble points on a map, revealing
where water flows and salt collects.
There are occasions, too, when boils
form on his back or hips, which must
be lanced: he uses a knife or an awl.
Relief from such conditions is,
however, temporary, not
because his medicine is rude,
but because all maladies persist.
Affliction is a constant force:
a blighted tree, a wormy calf,
a hungry child, a droughted land.
It is not merely man's poor lot.
Each day is full of sun and shadow,
for all creation; even kings
know imperfection: underneath
their snowy wigs are colonies
of pestilence, settlements of lice.

On the Property of Magnetism

A lodestone resting in the hand,
holding hard magic, some spirit broken loose
from a center point in the earth—this
leads to a stream of unanswerable
questions. What is the source
of tears? Where does all gravity
gather and what light does it make?
Who paints foxfire on the naked
floor of the woods? What
is the full history of taking away?
Is there a cave against sorrow?
What law commands the snakes
to shed their skins in places where
a man can find them? Is darkness
made from the pitch of fallen
stars? Why are a turkey's feathers
like jewels on jewels? Who feeds
the fire of the sun? Why are beads
better than gold? Why is a woman like
clover to a man? Why are some secrets
never told, as if they were beyond corruption?

One of Many Mysteries

My brother Squire and I
long hunting in Kentucky;
no place to stop and camp
along the Louisa fork:
the Big Sandy river
is a snake with three distinct
and twisted bodies. Night
had fallen like a tree.
The wind was boring hard
against us like a wolf
and we were deafened by
its howl. There must have been
a cave; we should have rested.
Our horses hung their heads
and walked without complaint.
The heavens opened up
and offered us a swath
of stars, a glinting path,
which helped us stumble less,
but that was all. Squire said
that sometimes God can be
a wheel that turns against
us for a reason, though
we'll never understand it.
We walked until the sun
appeared and the wind abated.
I never saw the cave
but I was sure there was
a wolf inside it sleeping,
a grin upon his lips.

Born Again

The darkest place I've ever been
did not require a name. It seemed
to be a gathering place for the lint
of the world. The bottom of a hollow
beneath two ridges, sunk like a stone.
The water was surely old, the dregs
of some ancient sea, but purified
by time, like a man made better by
his years, his old hurts absorbed into
his soul, his losses like a spring
in his breast. That deep baptismal trough,
my head immersed in a blacksmith's forge,
my eyes reflecting firefly flicker—
O nameless beauty below the stars,
O figure of a man descending—
I saw myself, an object of
decay, no speech, no sleep, a speck,
a weightless scene stuck in the eye
of ancient order. Mind you, not
a vision of the netherworld
or even death. I was like a seed,
a vision of a man who had
fallen into a second womb,
the cliffs above me stretching like
taut thighs of a woman giving birth.

The Wages of Dominion

I've had too many horses.
One horse shot out from under
my son, an injured look
upon its face. Two women
astride one horse. Nine horses
in a line, a scene of burden.
One horse, two buffalo rugs,
and two salt kettles slung
over the homemade saddle.
That horse died. We had
a bull. I made a sledge
from saplings. I piled the crude
device with our provisions.
I tapped the bull with a switch
and then we were moving.
The women now were walking,
their skirts tied up and out
of the mud. The land of loss
and fading promise lay
ahead. We had johnnycakes
and salted jerky for supper.
That night, another horse
fell dead. I fed it to
the dogs. The bull survived,
five hundred miles and more.
I've had too many horses
whose names I can't remember.

A Wife's Tale

Rebecca's life was one of several questions,
one after another, answered insufficiently.
Why do men become good at their cold
brutality? How do women bring ten children
into the world? Why are maple leaves so
evenly pointed? Such questions took too long
to answer, and after a while, she grew content
with the questions alone: Where is Fallen Timbers?
Is the milk cow running dry again? Is the butter
in the springhouse set? What kind of grave
befits a child? Are these rivers tinged with blood?
Am I a chicken?—like a girl's first prayer, in which
she sees God as a silver glass, all reflection
and light; behind her, a steady stream of answer—
but she went on, a cedar bucket in her hand,
her husband dragging through the woods like a boy,
her kettle on the fire, the look of wonder on her face.

Jemima's Idyll

A Cherokee named Hanging Maw.

A Shawnee in the river with a knife.
Three girls in a canoe soaking their feet.
Then the Shawnee pulling the girls
silently to the other bank.

Jemima's black hair hung to her knees.

That night, Hanging Maw's hands
on Jemima's head, his rough English,
his companions' gaping looks. Then,
her hands in his hair, looking for lice:
an unbelievably gentle kidnap scene,
full of artful delay and courtesy.

Three days later, her skirt torn off
at the knees, I find her threadbare
trail of broken sticks, muddied water.
I spring barefoot from the woods:
three girls sprung from the red belly
of an Indian whale. Jemima's funny
nickname: Duck. Our ragged life
of questions. My pronouncement
that deliverance is shaped like
the mouth of God. Jemima's keen
agreement that the world is more than killing.

On Death

The best thing about dying is it frees you
from the fear of death; you get it over with,
that fear you spend your whole life dancing
around, as if it were a fire and you were
a wild, ink-streaked Indian, kicking sparks
into the heavens. But death is not anything
like a fire. Death is like the wind: it is air
once held back and now released. Death
is not a buffalo calf half eaten by wolves—
that is an example of life. A man sleeping
in the dog-trot between two cabins, or
a woman raising her skirts in the weeds,
or a collapsed trio of hoops and rotten
barrel staves, the barrel no longer a vessel—
death is like these; it has a still foreverness.
I think of death as the king of quiet falling,
in that, dying we fall, maybe off of a horse,
or maybe into a daughter's arms, but it is still
falling, like a leaf loosed from a tree, never
to hit the ground. But once we die, the sense
of falling stops because there is nothing
that we are falling from. We become plain
stones in the bottom of a river, unnoticed,
life teeming above us, sometimes someone
peering down at us but seeing a face instead
of a stone, which is not death, but the false
image of death which comes from living in fear.
So death is the one who drops stones into
the water, shattering the image, as we sink,
and we look up from our river of foreverness
at life, painted and wild and scared to death,
and above that is a fire, bound by a rough circle.

Fancies

Unperceived, upon some eminence, you may enjoy the sports of wild animals, which here rove unconcerned lords of the field. Heavens! What charms are there in liberty! Man, born to enslave the subordinate animals, has long since enslaved himself. But reason at length, in radiant smiles, and with graceful pride, illumines both hemispheres; and FREEDOM, in golden plumes, and in triumphal ear, must now resume her long-lost empire.

—Gilbert Imlay, *A Topographical Description of the Western Territory of North America*, 1792

Sleeping in the Wilderness

No matter how well you dress the hide
a buffalo rug will always smell like buffalo:
it is a rank odor and wild, charged with old
glands and cud and the memory of running ten
winters, the last two blind. So you take your bed
in this way, raking dry leaves into a grave-sized
mound beneath you, pulling the mossy cloak
upon you and you spit out the last bitter cinders
from your fire and submerge your head, feeling
the dank fur on your face. And you try to breathe.
What good are the dim stars on such nights?
They only make heaven seem colder and farther
away. So you rekindle the dream about Rebecca,
in which the two of you are resting in the shade
of a sycamore and you skip a rock for her across
the river, and as you prepare to skip another,
she grabs your rough hand and puts it in her hair.
Then she lays her generous bones next to yours.
In the morning, you wrap the rug around you,
check your powder, rub some ashes on your teeth
and go to the creek where you wash all traces of night
from your face. You walk until walking warms you,
then you fold the rug and lash it to your horse
and you keep going to the next blue lick and the next,
the taste of salt already on your tongue, a precious
grain of civilization clinging to your brutal frame
like a pocket watch or a lock of hair; but you are looking
for an elk, or a bear, sniffing the air for musk.

Sheltowee

The women shaved my head with a mussel shell
and took me to the river to wash away
my whiteness; and then they smeared me head to toe
with bear grease and tied three eagle feathers
to the tuft of hair they'd left sprouting out of
my head like the earliest shoots of corn. And then
I stood in the sun all day until the grease
dried on my skin and I was red like them.
That night, Blackfish declared I was his son
and gave me a Shawnee son's name that meant
Big Turtle and took a stick and drew
my shape in the sand. How a fish could father
a turtle I didn't know; I believed,
though, it was possible, for Blackfish had
a skill with humble words, as if he only
had to speak the word and the air would make it so,
obeying his command. *Captivity*
is not the word that I would use when women
place a string of beads around your neck
and giggle to themselves; or Blackfish says,
You now have power over water, and when
you call the birds who live above the sun,
they'll hear you and rain will fall upon the ground.

Advice to Rovers

The service of a hunting shirt, a knife
whose heft is rightly balanced, a tinderbox
that fits the hand—necessities, besides
a horse and difficult geography
for anyone who seeks deliverance
from the measures of the world, the social weave.
Resolve to think in terms more loose. Make plans
to reach Missouri country by the fall,
for instance; and maintain your plan despite
impunity which surely will occur,
likely, in the form of rain or wavering.
The very crudeness of your scheme bespeaks
its strength. You will acquire the look of one
whose enterprise does not depend on gold,
which may include no shoes, long hair, and soot.
You can make salt; you can make peace among
the Indians. Do not disdain your lack
of native lights: you have the moon and stars
and fireflies dancing bright against the dark.

A Compendium of Trees

My favorite, the sassafras, whose leaf looks like
the hand of a three-fingered child, or perhaps
a turkey foot; the shape of an ancient letter,
but misinscribed, as if it were a writ
of imperfection; whose root
chews sweet and soothes a woodsman's aching tooth.

I fancy too the dogwood, stricken by
a vengeful God, whose bloodstained bloom is like
an eagle's eye, unflinching on its prey.
A tree that grows beneath the might of giants,
an urchin in the shadow of a queen,
a shepherd boy among the Philistines.

I've felled both oaks and poplars with my ax
and made a gunstock from the ash. I praise
such famous trees for what they yield, but I
praise more the haw, whose thorns are uninviting,
the Osage orange for its deadly fruit,
these humble chariots of wonderment—
may I be swallowed by their stubborn mirth.

Early

When the snares of winter get secretly sprung,
spring in this country cannot be withheld;
the season of rutting begins and redbuds can't wait
for bees to awake and birds now and then get
ahead of themselves and sing a summer song.
Such days to me are like a fifth season,
shorter than the other four, but far more wondrous;
it is a time of signs. One March, I smelled
like seven weeks of death and fire, and sprawled,
long rifle ready and meadow-edged, the sun
behind me rising, moving the line of frost
farther and farther away. My hope: some buck
would be blind to my presence; four kills and I
could go home to different delights. But then
a mayfly fluttered up off the grass, the frost
that held it nothing now more than dew; it heaved
itself free two months early and declared its love
for the air and nuzzled up against it as
a horse would a post, and I went home four short
of my goal, an eager flower leaning toward
the sun, knowing Rebecca would be surprised.

An Ode to Kinnikinnick

It is possible, I suppose,
to smoke most anything, but a stone.

A grapevine
is often fine,

and elderberries, I trust,
provided they are dried and crushed;

phlox blooms and corn silks and sundry twigs
and sawtooth briar stems if they're not too big.

But my Shawnee brethren knew the stuff
that burns sweet and smooth, not rough.

Tamped into a pipe of clay or bone,
kinnikinnick stands alone

as the substance, whose praises must be sung,
which fills the head with the spirit of the lungs!

A Comment on the Gentry

They have the finest horses, footmen, slaves,
and homes with blown-glass windows; their wives arrayed
in gowns, the acquiescent nursemaids tucked
away; the dressing rooms, the summer kitchens,
the entertaining season; fatted calves,
a manservant whose task is pulling off
the master's riding boots. The courtesies
of primogeniture persist! The law,
the vote, the plan, the new America:
all fancies of a rich man's mind. The life
of men who gild their conscience with the vision
of other men beneath them, is a lie.
They construe themselves as highborn leaders, but
they follow on the backs of lower men.
O, sons of planters, here is my passing
fancy: that a tribe of hogs would waste your fields;
your footmen pitch you from your stallions, and stuff
your mouths with common dirt and make you swallow;
that you may truly taste gentility.
Is there a law against such upending?

Ten Things to Say to Henderson

1. Col. Henderson, I've always believed all men are honest.
2. Begging your pardon, sir, I feel I deserve some compensation for my labors.
3. Henderson, I'm afraid I mistook you for a decent man.
4. Of course, you realize my efforts have come to folly.
5. Sir, I have a burden on my heart.
6. You must have known the treaty was a sham.
7. With all due courtesy to your honor, kind sir, I must relate to you that my affairs are in a dreadful state, which I fear your actions have hastened.
8. The Transylvania Company was a serpent scheme, was it not?
9. Henderson, you cur, I'll wipe that smirk right off your face.
10. My preaching brother says a willful wrong is sin.

A Study of Heft

A full-grown buffalo must weigh well
above an English ton. They turn
the earth to powder rivers, sixteen
feet across. I've seen four hundred
of them in one meadow. Traces
flowed in and out as if the buffalo
were several tribes come together,
each traveling different water.
I know the life of moving from
lick to lick. You follow one river
then another; you go around a mountain.
The level ground is in your blood.

Drunk: July 1787

Dust caught in the throat, a black cabin
full of anxious Shawnees, and the hot, still
night sucking away the bugsong in the trees—
reason enough to seek the sobering brotherhood
in a clay jug of Old Monongahela.
Men taking draws after other men, ragged sleeves
drawn across chins, amber drops in the dust.
I stab the ground with my knife and fold my arms.
A nameless Indian tosses a corncob stopper
into the fire and the room blazes into wild light:
glassy faces and the smell of old blood—
we are like one man alone, twisting his face
into a dizzy grin. All is well in the leaning world.
We smoke. I give a white man's cough and laugh.

A Recipe for Chink

Once you have felled and squared
and notched and laid timber upon timber
and allowed your cabin to assume its form
and leveled the dirt floor as best you can
and made a stone hearth and a chimney
that draws good air and given thought
to daylight and the likely direction of rain
and resigned yourself to living crudely,
you are ready now to render two bushels of salt.

Next make a log trough and fill it with water
as deep as your hand is long. Scoop
riverbank clay onto a hide
and drag it to the trough. Combine the clay
and water. Add to that confection
small sticks, pine needles, and threshings
if they are handy. Then add the salt.
Kneel before the trough as if it were
an ancient altar in the woods and knead
the dough lovingly until it is creamy
as a woman's hip flesh and you
are taken away for a moment by a small dream.

Compose yourself and take a plank and smooth
the dough between the timbers inside and out.
Resist perfection; content yourself with small gaps. Sunlight
will sneak through and give the dust a place to dance.
Allow unevenness to bring you joy.

An Appointment with Captain Imlay, Esquire, Dandy, Rake

I'd heard just enough of the king's good English not
to trust it—I hereby this, I thereby that,
I swear an humble oath—as if pouring honey
in the wind could cover up the stink of falsehood.
I walked twelve thousand acres for the man;
I entered the title and put my name plainly
at the bottom of the page. But Imlay's mark
had more curls than a grapevine: I had a notion
there was something hollow to the captain's core.
I heard he went to England and took up with
more delicate folk, hatching plans and schemes
in drawing rooms and parlors. I heard he wrote
a book of lofty claims. That's fine. But I
could make a different claim: a man's word must
wear breeches, plain and simple. And when you lay
black powder in the hands of someone wearing
pantaloons and stockings, you're doomed to fetch
a terror. Even a witless fool knows that.
I'd tell it to the king himself, I'd grab
his royal robe and give his teeth a rattle.

Wabete's Season

I never shot an elk in rut.
If he were making marks on trees,
removing antler felt, or curling
his upper lip to better sniff
the air, I let him be. I loved
to see one blow and shake the ground
with his desire. The fire alive
in him, the season of his fearless strut,
his yearly wound, would soon compel
my hands to drop and gently rest
my rifle on my shoulder. Keen
on making mothers, he would bound
away. I'd hear him bellow from
a farther ridge, announcing himself,
as though he were a king who needed
no entourage or introduction;
I'd smile and leave him to his pleasure.

Considerations: December 1799

My last winter in Kentucky,
Big Sandy country.
Deer hams hanging in the trees.
Rebecca's glow is fading.
Yesterday I killed four bears.
The moon is half, but bright.
I smell like blood.
I'm standing by the fire.
Our cabin has three walls;
the fourth is draped with skins.
I have a satchelful of voided titles.
I have a mind to leave this place.
I'll go to Spanish lands.
I estimate seventeen days from here.

A Description of a Dream or Premonition

Picture a gaunt man sprawled out
beside the weathered wall of a cabin:
he resembles a fallen branch,
a discarded arm of a tree.
He is barefoot and his toes clench
the grass. His face looks like
unbleached cotton. His eyes are pale
disks with candle nubs behind them.
His mouth hangs open, a black
cave into his chest. His arms
stretch into the air. Sunlight
speckles him. He looks like a pool
of water. His life has been a long ramble
with primitive beauty. He carved
a spotted fawn on his powder horn:
he doesn't need it anymore.
Blue butterflies come to him, one
by one. They cover his arms, they
light on his face. Their wings wink
back and forth. They fuss over him
as if they were washing a dirty child.
He now has the shape of a blue swarm.
The butterflies take his nectar,
his body consumed, his light dispersed,
his vision now disappeared.

Amendments

What in the name of Shadrach, Meshach, and that other one
is an *inalienable right*? Something
that cannot be taken away? An idea
not to be forgotten? Does there need to be
a written promise that a man will not forget
the teeth in his head, the hands at the ends
of his arms? The fact that rights get written
reflects the fear of taking, thus we have volumes
as testaments of fear. How about this one: the right
for a man to think of himself as a river
shall not be infringed; or a man's right to stick
his baby finger in a crawdad hole
for the sake of teasing, shall not be fettered,
or a man's desire to live in a tree shall not
be encumbered, neither shall any legislation
be passed pursuant to the hindrance
of the said man's woodland desire, despite
the misgivings of the general populace.

A Contemplation of the Celestial World

Whoever had the thought to render bear fat
and burn it in a lamp was touched a bit,
or bored, or left alone to ponder light
too long in some dank cabin: bear fat pops
and stinks and brings no cheer to our condition.
My brother Squire would burn such lamps to read
the Scriptures: eyelids smudged, his head immersed
in smoke; his Bible, like a gutted beast,
spread open to Leviticus; his lips:
a hammer and an anvil forging words
for prayer. Then I would go outside to muse
upon the many things which need no light,
the chiefest being tears and copulation,
then others, like remembering glad days
or moments which occur without regard
for stars or lamps—my thought: what matters most
is borne of darkness then makes its own pure light.

Pissing in a Stump

If you walk around the woods enough,
you start thinking; your mind wanders
just like your feet, just like your eyes,
flitting from one thing to another—
ground to sky, bug to leaf, sun to shade—
it makes you happy and for a moment,
you stop to wonder why. But you get tired
of the difference between a man and God,
the very notion of peace wears you out.
So you amuse yourself with trifles.
You count a salamander's spots,
you flap your arms and squawk,
you say, "I see you" to a fox.
The voice inside your head asks, Why
must every action have a meaning?;
just once you'd like to live a day
that has no aim. You spy a stump,
solemn as a minister, you peer
into its hollow neck, you relieve
yourself, you void your bladder
and your day, everything that matters
is canceled out, pissed away.

Letters from Squire

The natives came by degrees to be less apprehensive of any danger from me. I would sometimes lie down, and let five or six of them dance on my hand. And at last the boys and girls would venture to come and play at hide or seek in my hair. I had now made a good progress in understanding and speaking their language. The Emperor had a mind one day to entertain me with several of the country shows, wherein they exceed all nations I have known, both for dexterity and magnificence. I was diverted with none so much as that of the rope-dancers, performed upon a slender white thread, extended about two foot, and twelve inches from the ground.

—Jonathan Swift, *Gulliver's Travels*

Dear Dan.,

I have just mete with Mister J. Filsun late
of Penna who aimes to compos the booke
aconting our Travailes and bloodie warringes
with the Shawaneese. I tolled him but for Goddes
Grace and good Horses we survivd. He says now
the Britis have surinderd folke are sartan to move
West and Land in Kentucke will be ever more
Scairce. His Mappe of this contry is a faire
Renderinge but I mary his storey of this place
will be too Cherrye. M. Filsunes compainye
is a plesure notheless tho in Truth he lookes lik
a leetil Munky with a powder whig and I feare
he is to Delicatte for this rough Contry. I am
Proud to have a Bro. who has come to so great
a Fame as you. The tater bugges are verry bad
this Year and I have labord much pickin them
off but I sopose there will be a Crop faire enuffe.
How do you lik Tavernkeping there in Limstone
maye this Letter find you helde well in Goddes
Bosum, &c. and I remane ever yore Bro. and Sarvant,

Squire

Kind Greetinges to you my Brother,

Should you grow wearie of the toile and taste
required to maintaine yore diette of Beares,
Deeres, Coones, &c., may I recommend
you to the divers aplikations of bothe Swines
and chicken Fowl. The Husbandrye required
for ether is small and the Swines flesh
is posesed of much flavour and most
all of it can be eaten includeing the entrailes.
A Sow will produce no fewer than twelve
Piglettes pr. liter and they faten up soon
enough. A Swine is desirabel beyond its
common use for lard, soape, and the like.
Chicken Fowles are often of an ill temper
Espesully the Cocke but the flesh of sd.
Fowl is swete and the marowe in the bones
is rich and produces a good gravey for soping.
I knowe you are inclinned to yore Buffaloes
Livers and Tunges but a man need not travaile
seven dayes in the wilderness to hunt
a Chicken or a Swine therof he has more
time at his Fireside for recolecking upon
his maney Aventures. Plese forgive my
unsteedy hand as I am a tuch rumatic todaye.
Ever yore Brother and with Fondnesse to Reb. &c.,

Squire

Feb. 1802

My Deare Br. Dan.,

I Trust you have good Meat
suficent to last this long Winter.
My water Wheel sits idill as
the stream is froze fast, but
I have bisied my Self reading
Our Lordes Word takeing Comfort
in the Scripture I have also one
of the Qaker gazetts Which has
the Verses of a curios Britis Man
Who tells of old hunters and indan Maides.
He seems a Man who lives steepe
in the Cloud of his own Fancye
for he knowes litel of hunting nor
the fersness of the Indans, tho
I expect the Fancye is grate among
Temptations for all Men even the Indans.
My love and Godes Grace to you and
Reb., ever yore Bro.,

Squ.

Gulliver,

We felled a grate Oake todaye of which
had a portion which was holloed and full
of Bees. The Hive was the bignesse
of my Waiste and neerlye four Feet
in length. We filled six jug with Honye
which I marry will last us some Monthes.
The combe will make an hundred tapers.
We are as the Israelites and God has
give us a Plentye for which we must be
hummel Stewarts. Am I to understand
the Spanards have sold yore Terrytorye
to the French. What of yore titel and
Comands. Also we have found manye
Bones of the Mamoth as at Big Lick
which are grate in Size but of litel Purpose.
I am glad we never had to slaye such
a giant Beste. Hopeing you are hale
in these kinde dayes of Springtime,
I am, yore loveing Bro.,

                                        Squire

Brother,

My Tomohawke wound contyewes
to cause me much Greef. Manye dayes
I am given over to Alements, but
the Lord has Blesst me notheless
with good sonnes. The Gov. of this
Terrytory is a ferce Virginny man named
Harrison. He has sworne the Indans
to his fool-heartey Treatees and
I beleef Indana will soon be made
a state. We shall have no
Slaves nor bond sarvantes and I
am glad of that. The Indans
will be wise to move farther West
as all the Game is gone here. Oneley
God knows what Spoiles the Whites
Victryes will reep. I trust you are
hunting with yore olde frends and
in the loveing Hands of yore Chilldren
and God. Tydeinges to Reb. I am
yore Brother in Blood and Christ,

Squire

17 July, 1809

My Bro. Dan.'l,

I Pray you and yore Famly are faring well
in the Misery Contry. Ha! We will have a Plenty
of corn this year as the stalkes are taller
than a Hors and have many Eares on them also.
Tho my bones acke from our indan Scraps
I Rejoice in the Blessins of our God.
In the wall of my mill-house I have carved
on a grate Stone: I—Set—And—Sing—My—Souls—
Salvation—And—Bless—The—God—oF—My—Creation.
Such may belong more trulye in a Meeting-House
tho I reckon it suites a Mill since a Man
is but Gods Grist, his Lif and Death the grate Stones,
our God the Miller the One who turns the Wheel.
Do you have an Oak tree fit for shade?

Ever yore,
S.

Dan.,

What her you of Jeffersones kinsmen
who bucherred and burnt up a Slave
the night God so ferceley shook the Erthe?
It was two brothers and had been three dayes
drinking Likker. Man has made a heavey Burthen
of Woe and Sin to carye. I fear it is a sad
Tale. It is just as well you have got shut
of Kentuck as I do not knowe how
long God can with-holde his Judgement
on that place. Also what News of Floodeing
in your Contry? Praying for Goddes Mercy
on us all, I am yore loving Brother,

                              Squire

My deare Brother,

In all yore rammels have you not herd
of a Shawaneese called The Prophet?
He is reported to be some kin to Tekumsey,
the grate Cheef of sd. Trybe. As I beleef
all men of God shoulde be Brothers, I
am keen to meet this Prophet. He is said
to be Blinde in one Eye and posesed
of manye Godley Giftes. Should you have
the Fortune to make this mannes aquaintanse
plese enquire as to the wayes he prayes,
the Natures of his Prophesyinges, &c.,
as I desire to know the Manneres of his Faith,
tho manye of the Indans are hopeles Heatherns.
I continyue milling in this terrytorye which is
loathsome Flat but cherefull land for corn.
Ther is a vilage of free Slaves near this place
I have Prayed with one of them who seems
a good man. Manye of them have been verrye
sick. With kind rememberances to you and yore
Chilldren, I am, yore Brother,

                                        Squire

Apologies

The proneness of human nature to a life of ease, of freedom from care and labor, appears strongly in the little success that has hitherto attended every attempt to civilize our American Indians. In their present way of living, almost all their wants are supplied by the spontaneous productions of nature, with the addition of very little labor, if hunting and fishing may indeed be called labor, where game is so plenty. They visit us frequently and see the advantages that arts, sciences, and compact societies procure us. They are not deficient in natural understanding; and yet they have never shown any inclination to change their manner of life for ours or to learn any of our arts.

When an Indian child has been brought up among us, taught our language, and habituated to our customs; yet, if he goes to see his relatives, and makes one Indian ramble with them, there is no persuading him ever to return. And that this is not natural to them merely as Indians, but as men, is plain from this, that when white persons, of either sex, have been taken prisoners by the Indians and lived awhile with them, though ransomed by their friends and treated with all imaginable tenderness to prevail with them to stay among the English; yet in a short time they become disgusted with our manner of life, and the care and pains that are necessary to support it, and take the first opportunity of escaping again into the woods, from whence there is no redeeming them. One instance I remember to have heard where the person was brought home to possess a good estate; but, finding some care necessary to keep it together, he relinquished it to a younger brother, reserving to himself nothing but a gun and a matchcoat, with which he took his way again into the wilderness.

—Benjamin Franklin, "The Futility of Educating the Indians," May 9, 1753

On Being Raised Quaker

We were not the type to shake and tremble
though our garb was plain enough. We believed
in being quiet, the wisdom of not speaking
unless there was something that needed to be said,
such as a gentle reproach, of which I got enough,
since I didn't care for the plow or the loom.
(My father was a weaver; it's work well-suited
to the quiet type, even if you have eleven children.
And my mother, God rest her soul, was fond
of *thees* and *thous* and early on I knew I loved
the sweetness of her old-world tongue.)
But, despite their reputation, Quakers are high-strung
people and my older sister and brother married
worldlings, pursuing their fallible will, and, in the end,
The Society of Friends kicked us out. The timing was,
however, lucky, as my father was keen to move
farther into God's green creation. And, after all,
aren't we all worldlings, in a way? Of course, I've had
my scuffs, I've borne my share of sins, but to be honest,
I never saw the need to make my peace with God,
since I never felt we disagreed.

Bad Water

I was certain some savage upstream
had pissed in the creek along with every
manner of creature known to this country,
as soon as I drew the first swallow—mind you,
savagery is never governed by the skin;
nevertheless, thirst can make a man drink
vinegar, and I was thirsty enough for two.
I hunted three days naked because I got
tired of hauling my leggings up and down
every thirty paces. My horse had better
sense and patience: he waited until we got
to the sulfur spring—it was clean even if
it smelled like rotten eggs. I must have
drunk two quarts of that stagnation and spent
all day spitting sand to boot. Filson decided
to leave out the fact that I spent half my
wandering years with the scours; he said
it would be *indecorous*; but I say, a wanderer
is bound to make mistakes. Here's another
woodland rule: although they look like
the jeweled eyes of a deer, don't eat buckeyes—
they'll leave you with the tremors and sweats,
and the only cure is to keep a sassafras root
under your tongue and sleep four days
with your feet pointed north, as if you were
a compass needle or a crude symbol on a map,
and the buzzards circle over your flattened
parchment, as if they were concerned with latitude.

On the Limits of Natural Law

I draw in breath. My legs move.
My head turns, my eyes narrow.
My hand takes hold of a buckeye branch
and strips it of its leaves. The world
is all around me. The world reaches
to me like a wife. I put my weight
against it, my bones belong to it.
My heart is full of ether,
the air beyond the sky.
It cannot be touched, I cannot
lay it in the dirt. This conflict
is older than all the rivers.
How many miles are all
the rivers put together?
My legs will never know.
But my heart does;
and it is not a distance.
It is similar with birds:
the reason that they fly
has nothing to do with wings.

A Moment of Self-effacement

Feller of trees, I am an axman;
my ax, the dull thud of doom in the woods.
Long hunter of beasts, I am the lord of black powder,
my rifle a fifty caliber drumbeat,
tom-tomming among the valleys and bottoms.
The simplest machine am I, a low pawn of commerce,
a foolhardy ruinsmaker, bark and blood
on my hands; I move, ignorant of will, my soul
careless of the cloak it surely wears. Who
will bring me down like root and bone
to sediment? Who will leave me one
small particle reaching for another?
Whose dust will I become? These
wages I consider in October; the world
rains down around me and I look out
from a fireless cave, a mote in a sunken eye.

A Syllogism

A river cuts the earth the way a man
removes a bear from the realm of air and light.
Subtraction is a swift and clean event.
A river is the tool of God; a man,
the tool of other men, and like
a river, a man will find the easy course.
Our tendency to laziness is great.

A river is the child of other rivers;
a man, the child of parents—both depend
on lines traced back to some initial point.
Desire and water have the same design:
to grow, then move and flow; to take and make,
and leave, and want, then rest: to bend the world
to fit a purpose which is good, despite
the fact of loss.

The world is God's canoe.

"D. Boon Kilt Bar on This Tree, 1760"

It's true, I've had my trouble spelling easy words
like *bear*, though I've killed one with my bare hands;
and some men would have felt this was a feat
worth writing down, as proof of manliness,
but that is not my carving: history has
painted me as prideful. Another fact:
I took a Shawnee squaw in the winter of 1770.
I was cold and she was warm—much better than
a dreary cave was her fair lodge; she soothed
me with her sweet Algonquian voice. I never
told Rebecca and it was not a difficult secret
to keep. You cannot blame a man for keeping
warm. Besides, Rebecca lay once with my brother,
Ned, which I understood, one Boone being good
as any other. I was much obliged to that long-legged
Shawnee girl and left her the hides of two deer
for her troubles. The kindness of those days is not
recorded. We thought less of sin than one may think.

A Brief Religious Inquiry

The Shawnees must have twenty-seven gods.
My brother Squire has one. He says God's eye
is even on the sparrow. Could it be
a sleepy eye? My brother is a miller.
I say he should consider the god of corn,
but he won't. He's stubborn on the matter, says
he's never speculated. He believes
the god who loves the sparrow also loves
the corn. But I believe it doesn't hurt
to pray for water, trusty stones, and grist
to any god who'll turn away from heaven.

The Curious Manner
of the Antithetical

All objects and creatures possess their own secret,
and life, the sweetest draught, derives from the choice
not to tell. The world depends on such
restraint, the mastery of the basic impulse
and easy revelation. Truth evades
the obvious. A moral man will do
injustice, which suggests his goodness is
a cloak and consequence of something else.
Consider a man stooping over a fire:
he eats a rabbit with a knife; the rabbit
is draped over a stick like a rag; the stick
rests on two stones above the fire; the man
caught the rabbit with the same forked stick.
This is a commentary on purpose:
the man enjoys how small things function.

The life resisted is a great temptation;
it is the life of loving reason, the life
of noble documents and signatures.
But the rabbit is this man's treatise on freedom,
forged from the stick. Like other documents
it is convincing, a page of careful words,
but in the end it's rather relative:
the essence stays unknown. The man gutted
the rabbit on a rock. An owl was watching
from a tree. The owl will eat the entrails. The man
has made himself a simple creature. The man
is moving backwards in the world. He lies
down now to sleep with his feet to the fire. The owl

is restraining flight. The life resisted yields
another life. The fire trembles and burns
away. The trees swoon with deceit. Tomorrow
the man will make amendments before the sun.

Felix Culpa from a Precipice, 1771

Falling is not so much a danger as
it is profoundly tempting. The bottom of
a cliff is a society of bones.
The bones of animals and men entwined
as if one creature had given itself
first to the wind and then to the dust; a creature
of different habits and desires bound up
in one body: the head of a man, the flank
of an elk, the teeth of a panther, a fox's tail—
divergence made confluent by the need
to give. Brevity is just as golden as
eternity: that is the aspect from
this cliff, this altar rising in the sky.
Do air and earth deserve our praise? They do.

On the Season of Rain

I condemn the sky for raining six disdainful
days straight. I curse the swollen river, which
has swallowed axes and hides, forbidding me
to cross without a toll. A man confined
is like an oak tree cleaved in two by lightning:
its leaves are fixed and never fall. Loneliness
is knowing you are caught in the snake-eyed stare
of fate. Whatever fate it is—the fate
of staying put, the fate of moving on;
the fate of cinders, or the fate of fire—
the venom is the same:
a poison governed by an onliness;
direction, purpose, vision, need, reduced
beyond all argument, to one. No choices
to weigh, no decisions to make, no waiting for
the sun to rise as if the daylight will
undo your darkness. Soon the poison spreads.
The extinguished will is like a cave within
your breast. Your soul is hobbled like a horse,
immovable and mastered. If I knew
the word which is the opposite of despair
I would hack it in a tree and not forget.

"Old Isaac"

Your shelter is a cliff, or hemlock boughs;
your country unassigned to any map,
your days are wordless, but for a click to your horse,
a whistle to your dog, your hands rawboned,
your hair a thicket wild upon your head;
your sense of days is like a clouded sky,
and love a memory you loose like smoke from a fire.
You blow into your hands as God would clay
and give your favorite beaver trap a name.
You animate a blacksmith's vulgar art
and find yourself speaking to a jagged set
of rusty jaws, a mouth designed to catch
a squirming bucktoothed sacrifice and hold.
No wonder bends your brow, your simple faith
inspired by what provides. You savage trader:
you have become an Old Testament father.

To the Discovery Corps: May 23, 1804

Alas, what can I say! discovering
the Discovery Corps so near my settlement—
and such a humble one at that. Ah, well,
young men, I see you. From the shady bank
I see the prows of your clumsy boats. By the way,
if I may be so bold, what is the nature
of your adventure; do you seek knowledge, or how
to profit from it? The difference between the two
is not sublime, ambassadors. Tell me,
who has the spyglass, who holds the scratching quill?
And whose idea was it to sail up the Missouri River?
It sounds like another Jeffersonian scheme.

Though it does less good to warn the zealous than
it does to tell a drunkard that he's drunk,
I'll warn you just the same, O my Captains.
Whatever soars, be it the hawk or the plots
of men, must rise from modesty; a rude
beginning is our common seed. Consider
the farmer who has a mule—named Sis, for instance.
He hollers Gee, Sis! Haw, Sis! Just to cut
a furrow straight. An easily governed man,
so it would seem, a farmer who presides
over two directions and a handful of words.
But, surely, gentlemen, that's not the kind
of farming your Jefferson has in mind. I suppose
he'd rather cultivate beauty than corn;
and if that's what he wants, I assure you then
you'll find it. Beauty enough to sting the eye,
but not enough to make you turn away.
Despite its daunting scale, the West will make
you think that everything is reachable,

that everything—from a concept to a country—
is yours for the taking, so to speak. And speaking
of taking, I've known the sharper end of that
old iron-faced tool, but I'll not get into that;
such matters are beyond a man of my scope.

My experience with beauty is simply this:
it's thinkable as long as you can see it
away from you, but it disappears as soon
as it is under human touch or title,
and men will leave it as they do a home—
they burn their cabins down to pick the nails
from the cinders, certain that a man needs iron;
and whatever beauty beset that place is left
to mourn itself as it declines to dust.

Godspeed! I am amused. But one final word:
I know the mule is too practical for men
of learning to revere—a sterile brute,
you might say—but think on your boats, muse on
your keels, your oarsmen, without whom you would sink.
They bear you, they carry you as burden, friends.
It well may be a bitter truth but the truth,
as I'm sure you know, is beauty's mother—yet,
her child is always left to raise itself:
O, there is no hinge of fancy to your task;
your Jefferson is, after all, a man.

So, whatever trickle of river you unwind,
whatever glory you may grasp, it will take
you many mules to get there, many mules;
and some years hence from now, perhaps you'll see
the trail behind you, perhaps you'll know the vast
expense of blood and treasure for your Purchase.

An Apology for Unknowing

The shape death leaves on the face
of a man or a bear is not
worth knowing. Neither is
the crooked display of limbs,
whether or not the legs
were twisted or struggle was
a factor. Suffice to say
the end of life is full
of gore and beauty mixed
together, an alchemy
of pain and resignation.
Specific details do not
provide illumination.
I sometimes dim the lamp
of knowledge, forget the day,
and shut my ears to the news
of worldliness. Trade routes
open and close; mandates
are passed and repealed; treaties
are signed and broken; men
reside in parlors and caves:
such facts are nothing new.
I prefer the tyranny
of ignorance to the chains
of knowledge, if knowledge
will only be the slave
of triumph and pity, twin springs
of pride, of which I know
no greater darkness, none.

The Pleasure of Stasis

I wasn't always moving through the woods:
some days I sat like feldspar in a rock
fast bound to the world around me, or a wick
in wax, a candle's only vein, whose task
is waiting for a flame. But do we need
to burn to find contentment? Is life all light
and motion, or is there room for shadows, dim
and slow, retreating only when the earth
decides to creak a few lazy degrees
around on its hinge—as a woman clicks her teeth
in mild disgust and pulls the shawl from her lap,
confessing that the fire is enough—the earth
moves in two directions, like a gate
swinging open and closed with the pulse of the wind.
The fixed point must be the throne of life,
the regal seat between an ash and anvil,
reluctance and zeal. My point is we cannot
chase light alone; we must go back and forth.
One night a bear approached my camp
and I lay still and let him sniff my bones;
his nose against my neck was like the taste
of freedom; he took his paw and rolled me
over, as if I were a rotten log
and underneath a treasure chest of bugs.

Dryocopus pileatus

He introduced himself as an American Woodsman
and a Scientist, a thinking man who drew
from Nature—the bounty of the Creator—
and he was serious. I took careful note
of his fanciful plumage, his long red hair,
his green sash, his ruffled velvet leggings:
odd wear for a woodsman, I decided, but
perhaps the sphere of science is more colorful
than I had thought. He had a retriever and
a pea gun, a bundle full of dead birds, and a book
of pictures in his own hand. He'd made
a catalog of rivers and was keen
on shooting sports. So I barked a mess
of squirrels for him and we supped
as old friends would, swapping tales, passing
the jug, making what merriment we could.
Before sleep could claim us, he brushed his hair
the way a woman would. Nodding to the fire
I said, the bounty of which you boast, I fear
it will not last. He lifted a dead bird
into the air, stroked its red crown and gave
a laugh that I scarce could call a laugh.

An Elegy for the Moon

Why sing the praises of a man and make
more monuments to hapless human luck?
The lust for knowledge and action is just a ruse:
Who puts the common good before the idol
of the self? I curse the fame of human progress,
the callous lie of equanimity,
the hollow grin of charity. Is not
all invention doomed to be found out?
For instance, my long rifle warped under
the heat of too much lead; a good idea,
regardless of its merit, gets replaced;
another country gets discovered: time
is like a mattock at the root of man—
our human hands make fragile gods which one
blind generation worships, then discards.
Of course, I see the virtue of small
reward, the necessary means to reach
a moment's end, but I am glad the pride
of man is still short-lived—his fleeting zeal!
What laurels for the man who changes his mind,
the man whose signature is crude, the man
who is overshadowed by another man?
I dignify the need for lowliness;
a man is just a chimney made of sticks
and clay: he has a simple role to play
and he cannot fashion a plan for the world,
although he tries. I praise the man who fails,
the man whose mark is unrecorded or
erased. I praise the slivered moon, the rib
of frozen rock which once a month decides

to imitate the claw of a headless bear,
and without a ray of pride or guile
it rises like a specter and shames the stars;
I praise its ignorant swipe across the sky.

Opposition to Bridges

If a man cannot cross a river on its own terms,
then he doesn't deserve the other side. If he
is loathe to feel pulled down or set adrift,
or so cold his lungs refuse to take in air,
he's afraid to be a human waterwheel;
a river doesn't care if we agree
with its course or the fact of its flow. The same is true
for trees: we must go with their grain or else
they break—all thresholds and wagon hubs and flint-
lock rifle stocks depend on one direction,
which I call straight. Cold science has it wrong:
it is a body waiting and not at rest—
the root desire to move—that moves a man;
a bridge will take away the meaning of
the river and deny the love of crossing.
This is how to cross a river: strip,
and breathe, then feel the current in your bones;
forget that drowning is a word and sink.

A Description of a Crude Machine

There is no patent for a sorghum press,
no furnace forging away, no leather bellows
heaving and sighing to render coal and iron.
The union of shaft and hub is like
the coupling of a man and woman, they must
work together, turning one stone against
another. The great ash lever turning them both
is called Delight in Sweetness, which is powered
by a benevolent horse, content to walk
in circles for the remnants. Thus, stores are
laid in for the winter. Despite the going alone,
the single-mindedness, we need each other.
Fulton's folly was making a machine
that turns a simple man into a horse.

Notes on "The Natural Man"

When you get down to it, what does civilization
really mean anyway? Property lines? Currency?
Poor Richard's Piss-ant *Almanac*? Well, it doesn't
matter, because most people are for it. Filson said
this country could someday be a *polis*, a princely
city-state, he called it. The problem with that plan,
though, is once you get a *polis*, you no longer have
a country. How many buffalo roam around a *polis*?
And who has use for a dugout canoe in a *polis*?
I couldn't give a tinker's dam for a *polis*. I curse
the day I heard of turnpikes and tollroads. You want
the truth? I was rather friendly with the Indians!
It was the pro-*polis*ites who decided we should kill
the Indians in order to civilize them. I came here
a man of relative peace and all of a sudden it's wide
streets, evangelists, and courthouse squares. I have
no use for empire builders, or sweet-talking Jefferson
men, or any other citizen-swindlers. Every time I turn
around, it's a flourish of lapdogs and smart books.
What happened to salt meat and biscuits? I'm weary
of businessmen in spectacles and corset-hindered
women staring at you because you're wearing buckskin
instead of calico, and it doesn't take long before your
conscience gets sticky, as if someone poured molasses
in your powder horn; and now, however far west I go,
I've got three dead Indians on my soul: What kind
of civilization is that?

On Freedom

I never thought one thing was free except,
perhaps, a swallow circling a summer meadow:
and swallows come in swirling dozens, tossing
like a kettle boiling over a clover fire;
and each inhales an ounce of gnats and skeeters,
strangely free to each of them like salt or air.
Passenger pigeons are also free, as is
the wind-stirred wave of a scarecrow's hand, a kind
gesture from a sullen field of corn or beans.
And flint is free, and shelter in a hollow tree,
and water dripping from a limestone cliff,
a river flowing slowly, one drop at a time.
But none of this was the idea of a man;
he only wrote it down with bitter ink
and then amended it; his final word
was to take it back, his heart a broken treaty,
a paper promise torn in two and tossed
aside: man's chaff is well-recorded, but
the quill he used—from a turkey's speckled tail,
or an eagle's wing—was a gift from the king of the sun.

Testament

Squire's boys laid him in a cave for several days
granting him one final whim: that if his spirit
were unfettered by the earth, it might be free
to visit them and tell them all the wonders
of the other side. It was a tenderly
foolish plan, but death promotes such schemes.
Still, one will make provisions, and I have cast
my lot in that regard. One day in Osage
country I was hunting with Derry, my sole
companion now for fifteen years, and death
dealt me a fever which I thought would be
the end. So Derry bore me on his shoulders
and took me to a bluff above the river,
and I said, plant me here when I am gone.
But I love the God-made world so much that I
recovered to hunt again. Yet I know my days
are winding down; I will go and not return.
My estate is a simple matter to resolve—
I leave my rifle to whoever wants it.
Don't dress me up for death, leave me naked
and fill my box with mast: I'm taking seeds
to heaven in case God needs more trees. When I swim
the pitch-hewed river, bury me beside
Rebecca; and when his days run out of numbers,
bury Derry next to me.

Illustrations, Inventories, and Maps

Brothers—The Great Spirit is angry with our enemies;
he speaks in thunder, and the earth swallows up villages,
and drinks up the Mississippi. The great waters will
cover their lowlands; their corn cannot grow;
and the Great Spirit will sweep those who escape
to the hills from the earth with his terrible breath.

Brothers—We must be united; we must smoke the same pipe;
we must fight each other's battles; and more than all, we must
love the Great Spirit; he is for us; he will destroy our enemies,
and make his red children happy.

—Tecumseh, speech to the Osage nations, 1812

Feathers

Osage

Seneca

Pontiac

Elinipsico Mesquaki Allegheny Conoy Wyandot Paint Creek Tuscarora Sauk Petall

Dragging Canoe Kakawatcheky Ottawa Susquehannock Saucy Jack Sandusky

Pickawillany Catawba Oconostota Scioto Big Jim Attakullakulla Iroquois

Wea Potawatomi LoggsTown Manangy Mingo Shingas Tecumseh Sac

Manatawny Chalagawtha Hanging Maw Delaware Tahgahjute

Shuylkill Cherokee Watauga

Blue Jacket Chippewa

Nolanchucky

Piankashaw

Noamohouoh

Sassoonan

Kickapoo

Tutelo Seminole

Shawnee Red Hawk

Twightwee Nohelema

Miami Nanticoke Maquachake

Petroglyph

There is a difference between knowledge
and revelation: the former must be tested,
as if you hardly believe it's possible; but
the latter dangles beyond you like one
leaf waving on a limb, at the beck and call
of a private wind loosed from an unknown
direction. Another difference: the first has
meaning and the second pure existence;
which means war is the offspring of knowledge
and the end of war is revelation which is not
actually real. Chief Cornstalk told me revelation
comes in shapes alone, which I took to mean
there is no such thing as a graven image.

So this is the shape of a living man:

and this is the broad-winged shape of death:

and this is what happens between the two:

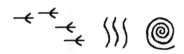

Small Possessions I Prize

dew claw from the largest bear I ever saw

powder horn

buffalo vertebra

stone blade from the Indians

rattlesnake tail with nine buttons

porcupine quill, stained purple

buckskin pouch full of flints

tail feather from a turkey

rock which curves like Rebecca's hips under my fingers

tinderbox and one patch from Jemima's first dress which I refuse to burn

a piece of English silver for a laugh

my mother's name scribbled on a scrap of hide

**A Rendering of What I Carved
On a Beech Tree in Missouri
Upon Hearing of Gen. Harrison's
"Great Victory," November 1811**

A Miscellaneous Inventory

Dogs I have shot:	1
Dogs lost to bears, panthers, coons, &c.:	18
Buzzards scavenging Ned's corpse:	9
Stones I laid on Ned:	63
Times I swam the Ohio:	2
Times I swam the Kentucky:	too many to remember
Elk I have killed:	6,046
Saddles I have owned:	1
Runaway slaves I have met in the woods:	7
Months I wore the same clothes:	31
Honeycombs I have plundered:	26
Cabins I have built and left abandoned:	11
Votes I have cast:	4
Children I have buried (excepting James—nothing left to bury):	4
Bushels of salt I have rendered:	2,450 (approx.)
Times Rebecca turned away from me:	2
Sworn enemies:	3
Men I have seen scalped:	13
Treasure I have laid-up on earth:	0
Nights I have cried myself to sleep:	6 (so far)

An Image of My Foot
Showing Blood, Sundry Wounds,
and the Ring of Sadness

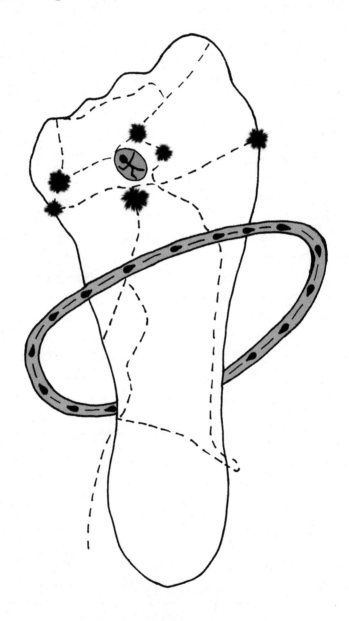

A Map of Heaven

Legend:

⊕ the union of all skins and peoples

░ saltlicks

★ the pathway to earth

🦌 the domain of elk and deer

🐻 the domain of bears

Λ the place where long rifles are buried forever

‿ the source of mountains, valleys, and plains

❀ a small fairy ring

🌲 woods and wilderness

ꞮꞮꞮ canebrakes

🍇 blackberry brambles

💧 the source of all rivers

🔥 the source of all fire

✕ the original buffalo trace

▦ the untainted shape of man

✾ the untainted shape of woman

⊞ the compass which proves all directions are one

🐢 the place of turtles

⌒ the place of all birds

👁 God has one eye and wings

NOTES

On God [p. 5]
However long the day, are we ever truly finished with the question of God?

First [p. 6]
Boone began his first trip to Kentucky in May of 1769. It is said that he and a handful of companions first viewed the rolling Bluegrass plateau from Pilot Knob in present-day Madison County. Of the occasion, Boone later remarked, "Nature was here a series of wonders, and a fund of delight" (Filson, pp. 51–52). How strange that Boone would use the term "fund," as if delight and beauty were commodities, provisions, in the manner of salt or lead. In the final line, "dark and bloody" refers to the legendary Shawnee translation of Kentucke, "the dark and bloody ground," which remains an apt description.

Without a Vision [p. 7]
Boone's second son, Israel, was killed at the Battle of Blue Licks on August 19, 1782. Boone and a group of nearly two hundred settlers had pursued a band of Indians and British soldiers to the banks of the Licking River. Boone worried that an ambush was afoot and cautioned against further pursuit. Major Hugh McGary, though, accused Boone and others of being cowards and charged across the river. Alas, Boone was correct in his fears and the settlers were dealt a resounding defeat. Blue Licks was the last battle of the Revolutionary War, ironically, a loss. For a full account of the battle see John Mack Faragher's *Daniel Boone: The Life and Legend of an American Pioneer* (1992).

The Meaning of Time [p. 8]
The earliest pocket watches appeared in Europe in the 1520s; the first ones were produced by blacksmiths and locksmiths. The science of measuring time is called horology.

The Sum Result of Speculation [p. 9]

Land speculation—or "development," as it is now called—appears to have been part and parcel of American history from the get-go. Surveying land was among Boone's various occupations. It has been alleged that he fudged a parcel here and there and that some of his surveys were riddled with mistakes, but, surely, such is the human condition.

A Possible Blessing [p. 10]

That natural things always maintain their nature is an issue long ago resolved. Whether man is a natural thing in the manner of bugs or trees is a question that still leaves us perched like a chicken on a fence.

Eight Analytical Questions [p. 11]

Whereas the Great Chain of Being has been supplanted by a more sophisticated cosmology, there is nevertheless something pleasing to its simple design; at the very least, it suggests everything is tied together. Even analytical inquiry, when it seeks first things, has a rhythm, an undulating pace, which can make thinking a bit like floating down a river.

Dog Day [p. 12]

Boone's name for his long rifle was Bar Killer.

Technically, a fairy ring is a blooming fungus that creates a ring when it emerges from the detritus of the forest floor. There is a lovely passage in book 6 of Spenser's *Faerie Queene* when Calidore first spies the fair Pastorella. She is standing at the center of several circles, surrounded by "an hundred naked maidens," covered in flowers—both a literal and allegorical fairy ring. It is a system of circles and beauty and natural abundance that seems to justify desire. It is a design of pastoral delight, which stops young Calidore cold in his tracks (see book 6, canto 10, stanza 8ff.).

That I Am Essential to Creation [p. 13]

Boone saw firsthand and at a primary level that there is a season when all things diminish. That the natural occurrence of diminishment sorely contradicts standard American principles such as might and growth is a circumstance best debated in a forum far different from the present one.

Schuylkill Country, 1742 [p. 14]

It is not known if Bye Baby Bunting is actually a game or simply an old nursery rhyme. It is true that Boone grew up along the then-Pennsylvania frontier with Delaware Indian friends and neighbors.

According to legend, Madoc was a Welsh prince who sailed to North America in 1170. He brought with him a group of followers and in time they assimilated into the native population and became known variously as the Welsh Indians, or the White Indians. Eventually, the English government invoked the legend in order to claim title to North America over Spain (our Madoc beat your Columbus by 322 years, etc.). Through the years, accounts of settlers and explorers encountering the White Indians attracted much attention. In the late-eighteenth century, there was an active debate in English periodicals over the veracity of the Madoc story. This prompted one John Evans, a Welshman with financial support, to sail to America in the fall of 1792 and search for the Welsh Indians. After two years exploring the Missouri River system, Evans had not found any Welsh-speaking Indians. He had, however, managed to make a map, which eventually found its way to Jefferson and on to Lewis and Clark, who, some years later used it with much success during their exploration of the Louisiana Purchase. Given Evans's route west—down the Ohio River from Pittsburgh—it is possible that he crossed paths with Boone who was then living along the Ohio River, in the vicinity of Limestone (present-day Maysville).

Part of the Madoc legend suggests the Welsh Indians originally settled near present-day Paducah, Kentucky. Boone's mother, Sarah Morgan Boone, was born into a Welsh community in Pennsylvania and probably knew bits and pieces of Welsh. The Welsh passage referred to is alleged to be the epitaph on Madoc's tombstone, which, according to an entry in the *Gentleman's Magazine*, Dec. 1789, translates:

Madoc ap Owen was I called,
Strong, tall, and comely, not enthralled
With homebred pleasures, but for fame
Through land and sea I sought the same.

Robert Southey published a well-regarded epic poem called *Madoc: A Poem in Two Parts* in 1805. However, few people read it today. For further details on the Madoc legend, see the excellent two-part article by David Williams, "John Evans'

Strange Journey" in *American Historical Review* (vol. 54, January and April, 1949), and Edward George Hartmann's *Americans from Wales* (1967).

Finally, while it sounds awfully quaint, it is highly doubtful that Boone's mother would have ever uttered the word "swanny," which should more accurately be thought of as a Southernism.

On the Whole, the World Is Level [p. 15]

Although it has precious little to do with this entry, in 1795, British prime minister William Pitt levied a hair-powder tax, assessing one guinea per year on those citizens who wore wigs and hair powder—arguably one of the sillier taxes in the entire history of taxation. As a result of the tax, the popularity of wigs and hair powder soon declined.

On the Property of Magnetism [p. 16]

In the end, is there a significant difference between a scientific principle and a natural law, between a fact and a force, between attraction and desire?

One of Many Mysteries [p. 17]

Of his ten siblings, Boone was closest to his brother Squire. They spent months at a time hunting together in the woodlands. Squire eventually became a minister of sorts and retired to southern Indiana. What they talked about in the evenings, how pleasant were the days they passed together, we shall never know, which is, in its own way, charming.

Born Again [p. 18]

The whole "born again" business alludes to the Great Revival, an evangelical movement popular along the frontier during Boone's lifetime. It is doubtful that Boone was terribly inspired by such movements. See John 3:3, "unless one is born again, he cannot see the kingdom of God."

The Wages of Dominion [p. 19]

There is no evidence whatsoever that Boone ever hitched a bull to a sledge or fed horsemeat to his dogs.

A Wife's Tale [p. 20]

On August 14, 1756, Boone married Rebecca Bryan. She bore ten children, endured Boone's long absences, and must have been tougher than old shoe leather.

Jemima's Idyll [p. 21]

On July 14, 1776, Boone's second daughter, Jemima, and two friends were kid-napped from a canoe in the Kentucky River near Boonesborough. Three days later, Boone and a band of settlers rescued the girls, an event that, because of its daring, gained Boone much fame. Later in her life, Jemima confirmed that, in fact, during her brief captivity she had checked Hanging Maw's hair for lice. Jemima's nick-name was, indeed, Duck.

On Death [p. 22]

Regarding Death and other matters, please refer to the fanciful Digression that commences on page 111.

Sleeping in the Wilderness [p. 27]

Though it cannot be corroborated by the historical record, it seems likely that a man who, for months at a time, lived very nearly like an animal, would have had occasion to muse on the pleasures of domestic life.

Sheltowee [p. 28]

On February 7, 1778, Boone was captured by a band of Shawnee and taken to present-day Ohio. Boone provides an intriguing account of this period in the Filson narrative. That Boone was adopted by Blackfish suggests that both men were ca-pable of seeing the interests and values they had in common, rather than quarreling over their differences. Despite the primal simplicity of such a relationship, it is a sadly rare occurrence in the annals of history. More often than not, the phrase "com-mon good" has been uttered with an accompanying measure of cynicism and deceit.

Sheltowee does, in fact, mean "Big Turtle."

Advice to Rovers [p. 29]

It is not known if anyone ever came to Boone and asked how to be a Noble Savage.

A Compendium of Trees [p. 30]

The largest sassafras tree in North America, which is some three hundred years old, is in present-day Owensboro, Kentucky.

According to ancient legend, a dogwood tree was used to make the cross. Fol-lowing the crucifixion, God smote the tree and caused it to grow crooked so it could never again be used for such a grim purpose. The blossom of the dogwood looks like a cross with a bloodstain in the middle.

The haw and the Osage orange, so far as is known, have no measurable value, at least according to conventional human interests.

Early [p. 31]
Upon seeing the mayfly in flight, one is likely to think the bug is drunk, though, of course, with joy.

An Ode to Kinnikinnick [p. 32]
While the exact composition of kinnikinnick is not known, it most likely contained substances which would be, by present standards, illegal.

Incidentally, in present-day Lewis County, Kentucky, there is a community called Kinniconick, nestled on the banks of Kinniconick Creek.

A Comment on the Gentry [p. 33]
For an account of Boone's firsthand experience with the gentry, see the following notes.

Ten Things to Say to Henderson [p. 34]
Richard Henderson was an attorney and judge from North Carolina. In the early 1770s, he and other business partners devised a scheme to purchase land in Kentucky and establish an inland empire, selling hundred-acre tracts to settlers. Henderson and his partners called their outfit the Transylvania Company. At the time, it was illegal under British colonial law for a citizen to purchase land from the Indians; it was also illegal to establish a settlement west of the Appalachian Mountains. This circumstance did not dissuade Henderson, however, and on March 17, 1775, with Boone as one of his representatives, Henderson purchased 20 million acres of land from the Cherokees, at the signing of the Watauga Treaty. The illegality of the situation was not known to Boone, much less to the settlers who had pledged their investment in the Transylvania Company. In addition, the Cherokees had no traditional claim to the land they sold to Henderson. The Cherokees received six wagons of provisions, weapons, and liquor as payment. Shortly after the signing of the treaty, Henderson authorized Boone to begin the Wilderness Road, the first established emigration pathway into Kentucky, a portion of which coincided with the present author's paper route when he was a youngster.

A Study of Heft [p. 35]
An English ton is the equivalent of 2,240 pounds. The word *ton* is derived from the

Middle English *tonne*, a measure of wine. Is there not a quality evoked by the image of a buffalo that is similar in character to, say, a cask of wine?

Drunk: July 1787 [p. 36]
By this time, Boone and Rebecca were tavern-keeping at Limestone, on the Ohio River. While he was hailed in his lifetime as a great warrior, Boone was equally capable of establishing peace and probably preferred it.

A Recipe for Chink [p. 37]
To compare the consistency of chinking to a woman's hip flesh nearly exceeds the boundaries of acceptability, even though, it must be acknowledged that certain kinds of labor often permit the mind to wander with great felicity.

An Appointment with Captain Imlay, Esquire, Dandy, Rake [p. 38]
Gilbert Imlay (1754?–1828) was born in New Jersey and became an officer in the Revolutionary War. Following the war, he lived in Kentucky from 1784 to 1785, during which time he hired Boone to survey and acquire land on his behalf. Imlay's business practices were questionable, to say the least, and he eventually left America for London and Paris, where he became, in short succession, a celebrated author of two books about Kentucky, Mary Wollstonecraft's lover, and a failed fund-raiser for the French Revolution (which involved the loss of a ship laden with silver and gold). It is believed that Imlay is buried on the island of Jersey, off the coast of Normandy.

Wabete's Season [p. 39]
Wabete is the Shawnee word for "elk," a species which was native to Kentucky. Boone left Kentucky in 1799, the same year the last elk was killed. In roughly thirty years, Kentucky's entire elk population was eliminated.

Considerations: December 1799 [p. 40]
In December of 1799 Boone, Rebecca, and a train of family members left Kentucky and moved to the Femme Osage region (present-day St. Charles County) of the Missouri Territory, which was under Spanish authority at the time.

A Description of a Dream or Premonition [p. 41]
We do not know specifically what Boone thought about the experience of death, but certain documents suggest he was not afraid of it, monstrous as it can be.

Amendments [p. 42]

It seems likely that the founding fathers did not anticipate a man like Boone, a man whose life, it would seem, demonstrates that liberty originates in the soul and not with a piece of paper.

A Contemplation of the Celestial World [p. 43]

Tears and copulation may be nearer to each other than is commonly thought. In a similar vein, the concept of antithesis serves a purpose which, truth be told, has its limits.

Pissing in a Stump [p. 44]

Speaking of veins, the chance that Boone would drain his main vein, so to speak, in a rotten stump, is not beyond the realm of possibility; neither is it unlikely that he would have taken from such a ceremony a draught of delight.

Letters from Squire [pp. 49–56]

Of his ten siblings, Squire (1744–1815) was most involved with Boone's adventures in Kentucky. They hunted together, explored Florida together (1765), and were involved in establishing permanent settlements in Kentucky. Like Boone, Squire was restless and later in life moved from Kentucky to southern Indiana where he and his sons successfully ran a gristmill. Squire was also decidedly more religious than Boone and was known to preach from time to time.

Squire's letters, muddled as they are, allude to the following: Boone's 1783 interview with John Filson and Filson's subsequent book, *The Discovery, Settlement, and Present State of Kentucke* (including the appendix, "The Adventures of Col. Daniel Boon; containing a Narrative of the Wars of Kentucke"); the earliest American reprints of Wordsworth's "Simon Lee" and "The Complaint of a Forsaken Indian Maiden"; Boone's favorite book, *Gulliver's Travels*; Boone's move to Missouri and his travails there; William Henry Harrison's battles with Tecumseh and the Shawnee, which culminated at Tippecanoe in 1811; slavery being illegal in the northwest territories (which included Indiana); the religious sentiments Squire carved into the foundation of his millhouse (which are visible to this day); the coincidence of the New Madrid earthquake of December 16, 1811, with the brutal murder of a slave in Kentucky by Thomas Jefferson's nephews, Lilburn and Isham Lewis (for an imaginative recounting of this event, see Robert Penn Warren's *Brother to Dragons*); and, finally, the establishment of communities of freed slaves in Indiana.

That may seem like a lot, but careful scrutiny of the historical record suggests Squire was a man who paid attention.

On Being Raised Quaker [p. 61]
It is true that Boone's parents were booted out of their Quaker Meeting in Pennsylvania for allowing two children to marry non-Quakers. In recent years, however, the Quakers have become more tolerant.

Bad Water [p. 62]
Scours is a rustic term for loose bowels.

On the Limits of Natural Law [p. 63]
That there is a limit to natural law, that there is a point when even nature is governed by a greater force, a more eminent design, seems to be at the heart of Boone's queries.

A Moment of Self-effacement [p. 64]
To be honest, "ruinsmaker" is not really a word and would not appear in standard dictionaries.

A Syllogism [p. 65]
That a syllogistic argument could conclude "the world is God's canoe" is utterly preposterous and defies the very tenets of polite discourse. However, there is a point at which all discourse must be said to wear the cloak of artifice.

"D. Boon Kilt Bar on This Tree, 1760" [p. 66]
Surviving historical records indicate that Boone would not have won any spelling bees. The matter and manner of Boone's "keeping warm" is pure speculation, although it is probable that Rebecca indeed "mistook" Ned for Daniel, since they looked so much alike.

A Brief Religious Inquiry [p. 67]
Is God watching? Is God involved? Or has God simply put everything in motion? It seems Boone was curious at least to receive a metaphysical wave from the Old Buzzard.

The Curious Manner of the Antithetical [p. 68]
In one sense, a human being is born from desire, which, although it has an obvious physical manifestation, is not a physical thing on its own. Thus, the inanimate essence produces the physical substance which, upon death, is transformed into inanimate substance, i.e. dust. While there clearly is a difference between the notion and the thing, such knowledge does not make it any easier to separate the two. Therefore, one may ask of the tides: Which is better, the going out or the coming in?

Felix Culpa from a Precipice, 1771 [p. 70]
The concept of *Felix Culpa*, "the fortunate fall," has been best illuminated by Milton. The matter of precipices, however, is more exclusively the province of Wordsworth. Often, it is only from a great height that we fully perceive our lowness.

On the Season of Rain [p. 71]
So bent on action, we have little regard for waiting, yet the natural world seems equally governed by both. A dry creek bed waits for water. An airborne seed awaits the wind. These are but two examples of waiting.

"Old Isaac" [p. 72]
Boone named his favorite beaver trap "Old Isaac," which, later in life, he gave to a friend. It is not uncommon for skill and craftsmanship to be employed in the fashioning of a brutal device, nor is it surprising that Boone made a gift of that device, as a token of respect or affection. In some ways, perhaps this is similar to the traditions of burnt offerings, blood on the altar, placing a penny on a railroad track, etc.

To the Discovery Corps: May 23, 1804 [pp. 73–4]
As has already been mentioned, in December of 1799, Boone moved with a large number of his extended family to establish a settlement in Missouri. At the time, Missouri territory was under Spanish control and Boone, having relocated—predictably—in a remote region along the Femme Osage River (a few miles above its entry into the Missouri), was awarded a land grant, as well as a post as a kind of justice of the peace. Both the land claim and Boone's modest bureaucratic rank were voided, however, when the region was ceded first to France, then later to the United States as part of the Louisiana Purchase. By May of 1804, when he was

nearly seventy years old, Boone was, effectively, a displaced person, and had been rendered so by the nation he had fought to establish.

It is true that the Lewis and Clark party sailed, rowed, and pulled their way *up* the Missouri River—a feat which would have caused a practical man like Boone to scratch his head. It is unclear if Boone actually met Lewis and Clark. There were, however, nine Kentuckians among the Discovery Corps, one of whom, John Shields, the "head blacksmith," is identified as Boone's "kinsman" (see Charles G. Clarke's *The Men of the Lewis and Clark Expedition*, pp. 53–54). In addition, one of Boone's comrades in Kentucky was George Rogers Clark, William Clark's elder brother. At the very least, it is certain that Lewis and Clark knew of Boone, his reputation, and his proximity.

Curious readers may wish to learn the following. In his instructions to Captain Meriwether Lewis, dated June 20, 1803, President Jefferson says:

> The object of your mission is to explore the Missouri River, & such principal stream of it, as, by it's [sic] course & communication with the waters of the Pacific Ocean, may offer the most direct & practicable water communication across this continent, for the purposes of commerce.

Is it reaching too far, therefore, to consider the expedition a rather poorly appointed and extended business trip?

In the same letter, but at this point regarding matters with Indians, Jefferson adds:

> And considering the interest which every nation has in extending & strengthening the authority of reason & justice among the people around them, it will be useful to acquire what knolege [sic] you can of the state of morality, religion & information among them, as it may better enable those who endeavor to civilize & instruct them, to adapt their measures to the existing notions and practices of those on whom they are to operate. [Reprinted in Frank Bergon's edition of the *Journals of Lewis & Clark.*]

Thus, in a proverbial instant, American foreign policy became part of the domestic agenda. That Boone would have viewed the Lewis and Clark party with a measure of suspicion seems only natural.

It should be noted that prior to moving farther in the hinterlands, it was not uncommon for frontier people to burn their log cabins and harvest the handful of nails left in the ashes; at this time, blacksmiths made nails one by one; nails were expensive and it was a virtue of frugality to use and reuse them from one homestead to the next. The timber, of course, was considered dispensable. I am indebted to Mr. Roger Rawlings for these significant facts.

The final one and a fifth lines of the current highly speculative document—"the vast expense of blood and treasure," etc.—are indeed attributed to Boone (see Filson, p. 81), in a different historical context, but one that could only be seen as prophetic. That Boone would make the distinction between objective knowledge and the economic profit gleaned from said knowledge, however, is yet another fantastical leap on my part for which I humbly beg the reader's forgiveness.

An Apology for Unknowing [p. 75]

One consequence of ignorance is that it leads to humility, which is every bit as valuable as knowledge.

The Pleasure of Stasis [p. 76]

Feldspar, a common mineral found primarily in igneous rocks, can make a rock appear speckled. The word has a Germanic and Old English derivation, which at one time may have meant "field sparrow," a bird, which is also speckled. Feldspar might also have once meant "felled sparrow," as in fallen sparrow. *Cf.* Hamlet's line: "There is special / providence in the fall of a sparrow" (act 5, scene 2, ll. 219–20); and Matthew 10:29: "'Are not two sparrows sold for a farthing? and one shall not fall on the ground without your Father.'"

Dryocopus pileatus [p. 77]

John James Audubon claims to have met Boone in Kentucky in 1810, when Boone was back visiting. Audubon's account of their meeting was published in his *Delineations of American Scenery and Character* (1824).

In order to "bark" a squirrel, the rifle shot must hit a tree branch so near the squirrel that the squirrel is killed from the concussion and, thus, the flesh is not damaged. Audubon's account of Boone's barking skill was borrowed in later publications by the likes of James Fenimore Cooper and Washington Irving.

Dryocopus pileatus is the scientific name for the pileated woodpecker, one of the largest and loudest of that species.

An Elegy for the Moon [p. 78]

Cf. Francis Bacon's *Novum Organum* (1620), section 42: "The Idols of the Cave are the idols of the individual man. For every one (besides the errors common to human nature in general) has a cave or den of his own."

It was not uncommon in Boone's day for a rifle barrel to warp after a long day of hunting, because the process of tempering steel had not been perfected.

Opposition to Bridges [p. 80]

It is likely that Boone never crossed a single bridge in his life.

A Description of a Crude Machine [p. 81]

A sorghum press, which is powered by a horse or a mule, extracts the sap from cane, which is then boiled down to produce molasses.

Robert Fulton (1765–1815) designed the steamboat. His first boat sank, because the engine was too heavy, thus the expression, "Fulton's Folly." Subsequent designs, though, were successful. However elegant its design, the steamboat still required some poor soot-faced so-and-so to shovel coal into the furnace.

Notes on "The Natural Man" [p. 82]

The original western frontier was a classless, remarkably heterogeneous society that depended on a combination of self-sufficiency and the barter system. It was not long, however, before empire builders and politicians and ministers decided to bring "civilization" to the frontier, thus dividing society, exhausting natural resources, establishing an economic system fueled by appetite alone, and imposing a legal system that promised equality while at the same time protecting the forces that at times worked ruthlessly against it. Though they had made "civilization" possible in the hinterlands, Boone and men like him were unwelcome in civilized society.

Despite his reputation as an Indian fighter, Boone is said to have killed only three Indians in his life, each in self-defense.

On Freedom [p. 83]

No written law can govern or regulate swallows boiling over a field of clover in the evening. Such a scene is a gift without strings.

Testament [p. 84]

In his final years, Boone's steady companion was a slave named Derry Coburn. They hunted together in Missouri, often visiting some of the Shawnee Boone had known under different circumstances years before.

Squire died in 1815, and his sons did indeed indulge his wish to be left in a cave to see if his soul would be free to visit them. If Squire's spirit did visit his family, no record of such event survives.

Rebecca died in 1813 and Boone lived with his daughter Jemima and her family most of his remaining years. He died in 1820 at the age of eighty-five. He and Rebecca were buried in the Femme Osage region of Missouri on a bluff over a creek. In 1845, their remains were moved to Frankfort, Kentucky.

By his last years, Boone had become a legendary figure, though he remained characteristically humble. He told one visitor, "'Many heroic actions and chivalrous adventures are related of me which exist only in the regions of fancy.... With me the world has taken great liberties, and yet I have been but a common man'" (Faragher, p. 302).

Sometime before his death, Boone had his coffin made. Occasionally, he would take naps in it.

Feathers [p. 89]
These are some of the individual Indians and tribes Boone encountered during his life. Blackfish, Moluntha, and Cornstalk had been among Boone's close friends. Each was murdered.

Petroglyph [p. 90]
These images actually appear at various locations in Kentucky. It is likely that Boone would have come across such rock carvings, which are several thousand years old. What provokes a man to carve creatures and gods in stone? Is it dread or praise?

For further reading, see Fred Coy's *Rock Art of Kentucky* (1997).

Small Possessions I Prize [p. 91]
None of these could be called "possessions" in any conventional sense.

A Rendering of What I Carved on a Beech Tree in Missouri upon Hearing of Gen. Harrison's "Great Victory," November 1811 [p. 92]
On November 7, 1811, as commander of the Indiana territorial militia, Gen. William Henry Harrison defeated the Shawnee under the command of Tecumseh at the Battle of Tippecanoe. Harrison was elected president in 1841, but died thirty days later from pneumonia he contracted while giving his inauguration

speech. The Battle of Tippecanoe effectively ended the Shawnee presence in the Ohio River Valley. The surviving Shawnee were removed first to Missouri and later to Oklahoma. The removal of the Shawnee to Missouri would have brought them directly through the region where Boone spent his last years. He visited them often.

A Miscellaneous Inventory [p. 93]

Of these, perhaps the most intriguing is the possibility that Boone owned but one saddle, for he was a walking man. Given his myriad expenditures, his outlay, his immeasurable personal loss, it seems obvious Boone spent his entire life in the red.

An Image of My Foot Showing Blood, Sundry Wounds, and the Ring of Sadness [p. 94]

On April 24, 1777, Boone was shot in the ankle during an Indian siege at Boonesborough. The injury plagued him later in his life. That the state of Kentucky is shaped like a human foot is certainly a plausible comparison, though it is not one Boone explicitly made. He did however have intimate knowledge of sadness and would most likely have acknowledged that sadness often encircles joy.

A Map of Heaven [p. 95]

That God has one eye has been alluded to several times in the preceding pages. The experience of being perceived by that eye is, quite simply said, like no other. Oh, the isolato! the one who hears that persistent voice at the center of silence. Could such a voice ever be resisted? Are we not always waiting to hear it?

★ ★ ★

Given that death is itself somewhat of a digression, it seems appropriate here to diverge, if only briefly, from our present concerns; after all, if death does not give us reason for pause, then surely nothing will. Therefore, begging the reader's indulgence, I must confess I am provoked by certain high-minded questions, which, I am keen to see laid, like so many eggs, on the table.

For instance, is not the primary subject of English Romanticism loss? Are not the great Romantic poems songs of sadness, the whole movement from Wordsworth to Keats a tale of failure, a lament, the sad recognition of an impossibility? While the ideal of Romanticism might have been to seek the balm of mankind's unification with the natural world, the achievement of such an ideal was never really possible. Wordsworth's long poem "Michael," as well as Keats's "Ode to a Nightingale," basically conclude there is always a fundamental gap between man and nature, always a separation; therefore, these two poems might be termed pastoral failures. It seems obvious that from William Blake to Wordsworth and later to Keats, one thread of Romanticism is a warning: if we sever our physical connection to nature, the human soul will be diminished. Such warnings continue to this day, though it seems a little late in the game.

There is also the implicit reality that most English Romantic figures (Wordsworth's Goody Blake or Simon Lee, for instance), were not so much partners of nature, as they were peasants employed by wealthy landowners, to generate a profit. In essence, *English Romanticism was not possible in England*, certainly not as a social or political model. There was potential, however, in America. What has Daniel Boone, and more generally, what has Kentucky to do with English Romanticism? The short answer is, quite possibly a lot, because the major players of English Romanticism were looking at America; they were considering American places and American people.

Coleridge and Robert Southey had devised a plan to form a utopian community in America, which they planned to call Pantisocracy (see Coleridge's poem by the same name, written in 1794). Their original idea was to locate in Kentucky (which they later amended to Pennsylvania, because Pennsylvania was where the British scientist Joseph Priestley had set up camp and both men were acquaintances of Priestley's son). At the time, both Kentucky and Pennsylvania were popular places for English liberals to relocate. In the end, though, the Pantisocracy movement failed to materialize; Southey hopped from one silly scheme to another and Coleridge found himself married to a woman he didn't love, whose most lasting accomplishment was to spill boiling water on his foot—an event that led to Coleridge's "This Lime-Tree Bower My Prison," a poem in which Coleridge is content to allow the imagined scene to serve as a companionable substitute for the real. But isn't Coleridge settling for the power of the imagination, great though it may be? Isn't the imagination a bit of a compromise compared to the authority of nature?

Perhaps because it was convenient to do so, Coleridge decided the mind or the imagination has more generative power than nature. This permitted his interior retreat and allowed him to avoid his unpleasant marriage, and more importantly, justified his movement away from poetry of hands-on experience to poetry of the mind, and, ultimately, to criticism. Coleridge's later poetry loses a sense of real place as location ceases to be literal.

In contrast, Wordsworth says in the preface to the 1800 *Lyrical Ballads*, "My purpose was to imitate, and, as far as is possible, to adopt the very language of men," and "I have wished to keep the Reader in the company of flesh and blood."

In fact, Wordsworth's great poetic growth revealed in *Lyrical Ballads* is the decision to make the people and places of his poetry as real as possible. But this was a challenge. Consider Wordsworth's earliest poetry, *Descriptive Sketches* and *An Evening Walk* (1793). Both are highly descriptive narratives, written in long paragraphs of heroic couplets, but neither poem elevates place or character above the level of the generic. These poems also suffer from a political moralizing, in essence, they are fables which give more attention to the moral than to the tale. Part of this is entirely understandable: Wordsworth was young, a student at Cambridge, and he had devout interests in political reform. He was anxious to be part of William Godwin's London circle (which he gained as we shall see) and had begun his visits to France; he also wrote anonymous political articles in the vein of "The Rights of Man." But his activism was ultimately an impediment to his poetry, for politics tends to depend on generalities and poetry requires specificity.

If Wordsworth's deepest conviction was that man should live with nature in order to elevate his soul, which would in turn improve society, then surely he came to realize that a political system could not engineer such a society. In fact, a political system, because it is fueled by external power, would only prevent the man-with-nature harmony, a system that is not concerned with power. Perhaps Wordsworth decided that man-with-nature harmony is only possible in a specific place and with specific people. This turn toward specificity is evident in his mature poems of the *Lyrical Ballads*. Let us recall the level of detail in his depictions of Goody Blake, a woman punished for stealing a handful of sticks, or Simon Lee, who is too feeble to remove a stump with a mattock. The characters in both instances are literally *touching* emblems of the natural world. There is a physical intimacy with nature in Wordsworth's *Lyrical Ballads* that is realistic and detailed and palpable, and the moral force that accompanies such intimacy is rendered with far more subtlety than in his earlier work.

If we can call physical intimacy with nature an aesthetic and philosophical *change* for Wordsworth, then is that change attributable merely to political disillusionment, a disdain for the ravages of the French Revolution? Perhaps that is partly the cause of such a change, but there is also a less obvious, though no less significant, possibility, and that is Wordsworth's familiarity with the American frontier and the character of Daniel Boone. A ridiculous leap! some readers may bellow. Well, well, let us see.

There is a stunning difference between man's relationship to nature in late eighteenth-century England and frontier America. In England, whatever relationship a peasant had to a potato patch or a coppice, was *forced*, it was a top-down political, social, and economic arrangement. (Wordsworth's personal experience with nature, it should be noted, was afforded him as a result of considerable social and financial privilege.) By contrast, along the original American frontier (in essence, Kentucky), man's relationship to nature was a *choice*, the original frontier was a self-sufficient arrangement and a Romantic kind of interdependence between man and nature was essential. We know Wordsworth acknowledged the limits of the English system, and most likely, he was able to see the relative merits of the frontier system. Wordsworth believed that, given the choice, man would live in harmony with nature, but he realized that choice must be available.

How did Wordsworth learn about the American frontier? Surely, there were many sources—Bartram's *Travels*, for instance—but one possible source, which has been too easily overlooked, is Gilbert Imlay's *A Topographical Description of the Western Territory of North America* (first edition, 1792). Imlay is best remembered notoriously as the American rake and opportunist who, after an affair with Mary Wollstonecraft that left her pregnant, ultimately abandoned both mother and child. Imlay's biography is rather full of holes, but there are certain verifiable facts: (1) Imlay had acquired title to several thousand acres in Kentucky as a result of his having been an officer in the American Revolution; (2) Imlay was in Kentucky from 1784–85 and made arrangements for Daniel Boone to survey and parcel out his land; (3) Imlay arrived in Kentucky via the Ohio River, landing at Limestone (present-day Maysville), a route Imlay details both in *A Topographical Description* and his 1793 epistolary novel *The Emigrants*; as Boone was then keeping a tavern at Limestone, it is likely he and Imlay became well acquainted and Imlay certainly knew that, given Boone's near-legendary status, land surveyed by Boone would be most attractive to potential settlers—exchanging his land for cash being Imlay's primary goal; and (4) Imlay got into financial and legal trouble, left the country, and left Boone with certain debts incurred as a result of his arrangements with Imlay.

Despite Imlay's disagreeable character, *A Topographical Description* is a remarkable book and was a bestseller in England during the 1790s—exactly the time period when Wordsworth, Coleridge, and Co. would have had occasion to read it.

The book contains all manner of facts and figures, from assessing travel on various rivers, to lists of flora and fauna, to details about the customs and practices of Native Americans. Imlay staunchly opposes slavery, is particularly sensitive to the rights of women, and condemns the English system of marriage, which tended to view women as property. Imlay includes several detailed and accurate maps, should an English reader choose to emigrate. He praises the landscape, emphasizing how its openness and abundance directly influence the laws, character, and morals of the residents. Kentucky, especially, is presented as a new Eden.

Imlay is even bold enough to dispute Jefferson on various subjects, such as Jefferson's judgment of Phillis Wheatley, the Boston slave and gifted poet who traveled to London in 1773 as a "sooty prodigy." Imlay includes a portion of Wheatley's poem "On Imagination" (a subject of great interest to the Romantics) and introduces it thusly:

> I will transcribe part of her poem on Imagination, and leave you an opportunity, if you have never met with it, of estimating her genius and Mr. Jefferson's judgment; and I think, without any disparagement to him, that, by comparison, Phyllis [sic] appears much the superior. Indeed, I should be glad to be informed what white upon this continent has written more beautiful lines.

> Imagination! who can sing thy force?
> Or who describe the swiftness of thy course?
> Soaring through air to find the bright abode,
> Th' imperial palace of the thund'ring god,
> We on thy pinions can surpass the wind,
> And leave the rolling universe behind;
> From star to star the mental optics rove,
> Measure the skies, and range the realms above;
> There in one view we grasp the mighty whole,
> Or with new worlds amaze th' unbounded soul.
> (see *A Topographical Description*, pp. 228–30)

The poem continues, praising Imagination and Fancy, terms that Wheatley uses interchangeably. Interestingly, the *distinction* between imagination and fancy is a topic Coleridge famously addresses in *Biographia Literaria*, chapters 4 and 13. It is worth noting, too, that Wheatley wrote "On Imagination" in 1773 when Wordsworth would have been three and Coleridge was one; if either knew anything about Wheatley, it would likely have been through Imlay's book.

We should be reminded that *A Topographical Description* was written for an English audience; it was widely popular in England, the first edition coming out in 1792. A second, expanded, edition came out in 1793, and the final, third edition, nearly six hundred pages long, came out in 1797. The book is constructed as a series of letters from Imlay to an Englishman, identified only as "My Dear Friend." Clearly one purpose of the book was to provoke emigration; Imlay, after all still presumably owned land in Kentucky and the book functions as a how-to for potential emigrants. Perhaps, though, an unintended consequence of the book was to provide fodder for the English intellectual imagination. The book goes to great lengths to contrast the liberal frontier American system (as distinguished from the colonial system) with the oppressive English system, suggesting that such liberty is possible along the frontier *because* of its "natural" location—that is, *away* from the original colonies, separated by the eastern mountains.

Of greater interest, though, is the fact that the second and third editions include as a rather curious appendix, the entirety of John Filson's 1784 book, *The Discovery, Settlement and Present State of Kentucke*, which has its own appendix: "The Adventures of Col. Daniel Boon; containing a Narrative of the Wars of Kentucke." The Boone "autobiography" begins with this sentence: "Curiosity is natural to the soul of man, and interesting objects have a powerful influence on our affections"— rather a Romantic notion, some fourteen years before the publication of *Lyrical Ballads*. The narrative covers Boone's life from his first entry into Kentucky in 1769 to 1783, the date that Filson interviewed Boone for his book. Whether or not the Boone narrative is wholly true or in any way resembles Boone's actual voice is a matter of debate. It is generally assumed, though, that the narrative is faithful in spirit to the actual events of Boone's life during these years.

By including the Boone narrative in the later editions of *A Topographical Description*, Imlay offers an English audience not simply a general informative description but a specific, honestly rendered, and presumably true story: it puts a real person and a real place together, with lots of details and adventures, and draws the conclusion that man and nature belong to each other. In effect, the Boone narrative puts the reader, as Wordsworth says, "in the company of flesh and blood" and focuses, much as the *Lyrical Ballads* do, on "incidents and situations from common life...whereby ordinary things should be presented to the mind in an unusual aspect" (see the 1800 preface). The narrative contains accounts of Boone's "captivity," carefully noting that he was adopted by the Shawnee. Also included is Boone's dramatic rescue of his daughter, Jemima, and two other girls, who had been kidnapped by Indians—an event which made Boone famous. Aside from the sheer adventure of the events, the narrative gives the reader a sense of what the wilderness is like and how Boone is affected by being in the wilderness: despite loss and hardship, he now lives in "peace and safety, enjoying the sweets of liberty, and the bounties of Providence." The idea that human suffering could be redeemed by nature is one of Wordsworth's touchstones, and a notion that spurred him in 1795 to part company with cool-hearted Godwinism and politics in general.

In addition to the content of the narrative, the very style and tone of the "writing" (the quotes are added since, presumably, the narrative is Filson's transcription of his interview with Boone) must have appealed to Wordsworth's poetic ear. Consider these passages from the narrative which present Wordsworthian notions in an authentic American frontier voice:

> Thus situated, many hundred miles from our families in the howling wilderness, I believe few would have equally enjoyed the happiness we experienced. I often observed to my brother [Squire], You see how little nature requires to be satisfied. Felicity, the companion of content, is rather found in our own breasts than in the enjoyment of external things: And I firmly believe it requires but a little philosophy to make a man happy in whatsoever state he is. (p. 53)

> Thus I was surrounded with plenty in the midst of want. I was happy in the midst of dangers and inconveniences. In such a diversity it was impossible I should be disposed to melancholy. No populous city, with all the varieties of commerce and stately structures, could afford so much pleasure to my mind, as the beauties of nature I found here. (p. 56)

> Two darling sons, and a brother, have I lost by savage hands, which have also taken from me forty valuable horses, and abundance of cattle. Many dark and sleepless nights have I been a companion for owls [see Job 30:29, KJV], separated from the chearful [sic] society of men, scorched by the Summer's sun, and pinched by the Winter's cold, an instrument ordained to settle the wilderness. But now the scene is changed: Peace crowns the sylvan shade. (pp. 80–81)

The curious reader will note the highly iambic cadence of the final passage above—surely another feature that would have attracted Wordsworth and other budding Romantics. The above passages also provide a kind of imagery that Wordsworth used consistently: the image of the individual *isolated* in the natural world.

If ever there were a Noble Savage, surely it is Boone.

Was English Romanticism imported from the American frontier by the likes of Gilbert Imlay, a smooth-talking scoundrel? Is the barely literate yeoman Daniel Boone the quintessential Romantic character? Is Kentucky the ideal Romantic landscape? To better appreciate the plausibility of such questions, we must learn more of Imlay's brief ascent as a literary fixture in mid-1790s London and of the very real possibility that he and Wordsworth crossed paths.

That the early Romantics considered America for aesthetic and philosophical concerns seems obvious. W. M. Verhoven and Amanda Gilroy, for instance, establish that Coleridge carefully read Imlay's *A Topographical Description* as research for the ill-fated Pantisocracy endeavor (see their engaging introduction to the 1998 reissue of Imlay's *The Emigrants*). A clear link between Imlay and Wordsworth, though, is William Godwin, the writer, political philosopher, and guru to younger English radicals during the mid-1790s, a man whose ideas and person would have attracted both Wordsworth and Imlay.

In his masterful and voluminous *The Hidden Wordsworth* (1998), Kenneth Johnston provides thorough proof of Wordsworth's early political interests, particularly his activities as a journalist. Much of Wordsworth's life in the early-to-mid-1790s (essentially until the publication of *Lyrical Ballads*) is a bit vague, because, as Johnston says, Wordsworth was rather adept at "erasing unwanted items from the curriculum vitae of his radical youth" (p. 452). It is certain, though, that Wordsworth and Imlay had much in common in this time period: (1) they knew many of the same people and had similar political interests and ambitions; (2) both men shuttled back and forth between London and Paris as observers and supporters of the French Revolution; and (3) both men fathered children out of wedlock— Wordsworth with Annette Vallon (Caroline was born in December of 1792) and Imlay with Mary Wollstonecraft (Fanny was born in April of 1794)—and both men, whether due to circumstance or choice is debatable, abandoned mother and child. Essentially, both Wordsworth and Imlay were engaged in passionate, ambitious, dangerous, and potentially treasonous schemes.

In the interest of brevity, then, let us turn our attention to a significant and previously unconsidered possible alliance between Wordsworth and Imlay, by way of Wordsworth's partnership with William Mathews and their obscure and anonymous publishing venture, an eight-page political gazette known as *The Philanthropist*.

The Philanthropist was printed by Daniel Isaac Eaton nearly weekly from the spring of 1795 to early 1796. Johnston suggests it is likely that at least certain entries bear the influence of Godwin and other mature political thinkers, and also identifies several articles and poems in the various issues that appear to be the work of Wordsworth's mind, if not of his hand (427–67). Of special interest is the twenty-third issue, which was published August 31, 1795, and which includes the following poem from the pen of a poet identified as "Clericus":

LINES,

Addressed to the Editor of the Philanthropist,
on contrasting it with the general History of this Country,
and the Writers of the present Day in particular.

BEFRIEND me Night, best patroness of grief,
 Over the pole thy thickest mantle throw,
And work my flatter'd fancy to belief;
 My sorrows are too dark for day to know.
  The leaves should all be black wheron I write,
  And letters where my tears have wash'd the spaces white.

While I unfold the red historic page,
 Where all my country's losses deep are stain'd
In bloody deeds, which neither youth or age
 Will consecrate to honour, loss'd or gain'd;
  And whilst I mourn the battles fought and won
  By Pichegru, the victorious France's valiant son.

Pichegru, whose name in arms thro' Europe rings,
 Filling her jealous Monarchs with amaze,
And rumours loud that daunt despotic kings,
 Food to each mouth for energy or for praise.

Thy firm undaunted valour ever forms
The safety of the state—tho' loft with storms.

The twinkling stars assist my willing tasks,
    And lulling winds to study fit the mind;
But the still breath of night with boldness asks,
    Are such events a blessing to mankind?
        I weep a flood of tears, and close the book,
        Presenting death and horror at each look.

But yet instruction seals the blood stain'd page,
    We there behold the conquest Freedom gains
O'er Kings and Nobles, pow'r and priestly rage,
    A noble conquest tho' the page it stains;
        Since liberty to man, and every right
        Follows the train of battles which they fight.

But, Ah! such scenes delight the men alone,
    Who void of love to man, and fond of war,
Made dupes by Princes to support the throne,
    That rules by rapine and continual jar,
        For what can War but endless War still breed,
        Till truth and right from violence be freed.

The philanthropic mind forbears to tell
    The carnage, death and slaughter that attend
Contending armies, and the hideous yell,
    Which men, half dead, from mangled bodies send,
        And dropping one sad tear on hist'ry's page,
        Forbear to grieve since better times presage.

Again I take the writings to my hand
    Of Patriot Eaton "Philanthropic" call'd,
I read with pleasure—and my native land
    Reaps profit too—and Tyrants are appall'd,
        Continue your exertions in the People's Cause;
        And every Patriot will rejoin applause.

While Johnston suggests that Clericus might well be Wordsworth's friend, Francis Wrangham, he notes that certain passages from "Lines" bear strong resemblance in subject matter and wording to various sections of Wordsworth's "Salisbury Plain" (see Johnston, pp. 450–51; the curious reader might also consult *The Prelude*, book v, ll. 1–49). By August 1795, Wordsworth had seen his share of bloodshed spawned by the French Revolution and its descent into terror, which is echoed in "Lines." In addition, the steady meter of these lines, as well as the classical stanza, suggest the work of a poet-in-training, which fits Wordsworth. Finally, the poem bears an interesting resemblance to "Lines Written in Early Spring" (published in the 1798 *Lyrical Ballads*), whose refrain "What man has done to man" is similar in spirit to the above "men alone, / Who void of love to man."

Now we come to the linchpin of our present argument. The very next issue of *The Philanthropist*, September 7, 1795, contains the following poem:

AN ODE TO KENTUCKY,

BY AN EMIGRANT

Hail modern Eden!—hail thy blooming sweets!
Thy promis'd favours, and thy fragrance, greets
My ardent wishes to salute thy plains,
And plant thy meadows with European grains.
Hail happy spot! that yields thy sweets profuse,
To waste in air, or rot in morning dews
Uncultivated—unenjoy'd by Man,
Reserv'd for latter ages in th' Almighty's plan.
No longer let thy fertile region waste
Its fruit (spontaneous fitted for the taste),
But let me now thy proffer'd sweets caress,
Thy rich profusion taste, thy meads possess.
May heav'n inspire a train of honest swains,
To emigrate, and cultivate thy plains,
And prove in earnest, what was said before,
That Eden now, is what in days of yore
It was to Adam, 'ere the Garden fence
Had felt a breach from Satan's impudence.
May many sons of Freedom catch the fire,

And from those guilty madd'ing scenes retire,
(Which now envelope Europe more and more,
And threaten judgments on Great Britain's shore)
To those sweet Arbours in Kentucky's grant,
Whose rich production will supply each want;
Whose ample resources, with little toil,
Will crown their labours, and their cares beguile.
No taxes there oppress the lab'ring kind,
No tyrant Kings in chains their slaves to bind;
There are no game laws to prevent a man
From shooting hares, or pheasants if he can,
The Rivers there are free as we can wish,
And every man may catch a dish of fish.
No laws of primogeniture, to wrong
The most uncar'd for infant of the throng;
There are no lazy Parsons, who demand
The tenth of all the produce of the land;
Nor Pope, nor Bishop, to enslave the mind,
But all may liberty of conscience find.
No Burke's, no Pitt's, no Windham's, nor Dundas's,
To stigmatize you all as swine or asses;
There is no tax for "apeing your superiors,"
For all are equal there, and none inferiors.
There are no Nabobs, who from Indian plunder
Return, and fill their neighbours all with wonder;
No pamper'd hosts of pensioners you'll find,
To live upon th' industry of mankind.
No hireling spies, nor foul informers there,
To herd amongst you, merely to ensnare;
No harden'd crimps in government employ,
To steal your children, or your youths decoy.
No prostitution stains that happy clime,
Because no Prince to patronize the crime;
But every man may there in peace combine,
Those blessings which Heav'n did for all design;
And whensoever death shall call him hence,

He leaves his progeny a competence.
Then hasten to Kentucky's fruitful soil,
Nor longer in European fetters toil;
Possess this land of liberty and plenty,
And say "the despots of the earth have sent ye."

Imlay's familiarity with the subject matter and the coincidence of "Emigrant" with the title of his 1793 novel are virtually incontrovertible proof that Imlay is also the poet. Furthermore, the escapism expressed in the "Ode" is a sentiment both Imlay and Wordsworth would have felt during this time. In fact, Wordsworth had left London in August of 1795, amid fears that his circle had been infiltrated by government spies and after coming to terms with his fundamental disagreement with Godwinism. Imlay was in hardly better shape, having lost much of his money to a crooked Swedish ship captain. By this point, retreat must have been desirable, and that is exactly what both men did: Imlay retreating into historical obscurity and Wordsworth retreating to the countryside and poetry.

Just as Wordsworth had reason to suppress his relationship with Annette Vallon; the birth of their daughter, Caroline; and his political activities of the mid-1790s, he probably also had reason to suppress any connection he might have had to Imlay. Imlay's intrigues were likely far more dangerous, outlandish, and punishable than Wordsworth's, and any connection to Imlay might have led to guilt by association. Furthermore, by 1796, Imlay's name was pretty much mud, thanks to the publication of Mary Wollstonecraft's *A Short Residence in Sweden, Norway, and Denmark* and later, in 1798, William Godwin's *Memoirs of the Author of "The Rights of Woman."* As we have noted, Wordsworth's record has been carefully sanitized (clearly by his own efforts and perhaps unwittingly by Wordsworth scholars through the years), and while it is likely that Wordsworth finally rejected Imlay the person, he might have nevertheless retained certain images and ideas from Imlay the writer.

Let us briefly consider the significant changes that appear in Wordsworth's poetry after August of 1795, in particular, the *Lyrical Ballads* of 1798. There are two poems in *Lyrical Ballads* that are set at least partly in North America—"The Female Vagrant" and "The Complaint of a Forsaken Indian Woman." The "Female Vagrant" has sailed to America with her soldier husband only to have her entire family die "by sword / And ravenous plague" (ll. 132–33). In subsequent revisions, "The Female Vagrant" is absorbed into the much longer "Salisbury Plain," which can now be seen as a precursor to relevant passages in *The Prelude* and a summary of Wordsworth's personal and political experiences of the mid-1790s. The Indian woman has her child taken from her and she is left in the wilderness to die. Both poems expose the moral failure that occurs when human sympathy is withheld, when political and rational expediency overrule compassion. While this is clearly one of Wordsworth's grievances with Godwin, it is also significant that Boone is presented in the narrative Imlay borrowed from Filson as a man of great sympathy and a man who experienced great personal loss. Had Wordsworth known Imlay and recognized that Imlay was rather unsympathetic toward Mary Wollstonecraft and their daughter, he surely would have seen the moral contrast between Imlay and Boone, which would have further elevated Boone in Wordsworth's imagination as a man who took moral guidance not from other men, but from Nature. This brings us to one of Wordsworth's best poems, "Simon Lee, the Old Huntsman," which presents a man who has lived his life in direct contact with the natural world. Wordsworth implies Simon is morally upright and capable of gratitude because of his contact with Nature. Despite Wordsworth's later gloss that the poem refers to a local man, it is nevertheless curious to note the metrical similarity between the names Simon Lee and Daniel Boone—a noble old huntsman himself. Curiously, "Simon Lee" was one of Wordsworth's first American publications, appearing as a reprint in the Philadelphia-based *Port Folio* in 1801, which had a Quaker affiliation (see Joel Pace's *The Reception and Influence of the "Lyrical Ballads" in America*, 1998).

One final note on Capt. Imlay. The curious reader may be interested to learn that Edith Franklin Wyatt, in an October 1929 article in the *Atlantic Monthly*, identifies Imlay's *The Emigrants* (1793) as the "first American novel"—which was, ironically, written and published in England. Ms. Wyatt quotes Imlay's preface to the novel, in which he says, "'In this history I have scrupulously attended to natural circumstances and the manners of the day; and in every particular I have had a real character for my model.'" This sounds much like Wordsworth's preface to the 1800 *Lyrical Ballads*. Wyatt continues her praise for the novel, noting that, aside from the partly political and partly silly domestic issues in the plot, the novel reveals "the beauty of a genuine love of freedom, the fascination of the air of virgin country" and displays "the author's passion for the wild land, its streams, valleys, mountain forests, and wide-spreading high prairies." Wyatt further quotes a letter from Mary Wollstonecraft to her sister, Everina, during the early days of her attachment to Imlay, in which Wollstonecraft says of Imlay, "'Having been brought

up in the interior parts of America, he is the most natural, unaffected creature.'"
Almost in the same breath, Wyatt quotes the Boone narrative which Imlay borrowed from Filson to include in the latter editions of *A Topographical Description*—
"'Curiosity is natural to the soul of man,'" etc.—suggesting that to the English radicals of the 1790s, almost anyone who had been brought up in the "interior parts of America" would have had the allure of being a "natural, unaffected creature," especially, our man Boone.

Alas, there is no tangible proof that Wordsworth and Imlay were acquaintances or even collaborators. It is, however, almost certain that they knew each other, and, especially given Imlay's initial popularity as an American writer who had lived in the American backwoods, it is likely that Wordsworth would have read Imlay carefully, gleaning a feeling for Kentucky's wilderness landscape and a sense of the flesh and blood of Daniel Boone. It is certain that Wordsworth came to value the hands-on experience of Man-in-Nature over political parlor talk. Boone was a living example of the synthesis of mental and physical experience, which is both natural and humane, and which became Wordsworth's primary aesthetic.

As a parting footnote, the curious reader may wish to know that other figures from the Romantic era also had connections to Kentucky and Boone. Had they married, Mary Wollstonecraft and Imlay planned to emigrate to America, possibly Kentucky, and live on a farm (see C. Kegan Paul's 1879 edition of *Mary Wollstonecraft, Letters to Imlay* and Godwin's *Memoirs of the Author of "The Rights of Woman"*). We have already mentioned the Coleridge-Southey flirtation with Kentucky during their Pantisocracy phase.

The Kentucky-Romanticism connection also continues into the second generation of English Romantics. John Keats's brother, George, emigrated to Kentucky in 1818 with his bride—"to the wild regions beyond the Alleghanies"—where he settled in Louisville and eventually ran a flour mill and lumberyard (see "George Keats" in the April 1843 issue of *The Dial*, edited, incidentally, by Ralph Waldo Emerson). George's emigration is a decision Keats supported, as evidenced in his letter to Benjamin Bailey on May 28, 1818, in which he refers to his brother's "resolution to emigrate to the back Settlements of America, become a Farmer and work with his own hands...[because] he is of too independent and liberal a Mind to get on in Trade in this Country" [England]. Curiously, George Keats also entered into a failed riverboat scheme with John James Audubon, the naturalist (also writing for an English audience), a man who knew Boone (see Audubon's *Delineations of American Scenery and Character*, 1824). Of the Audubon business tangle,

Keats writes to George, "Tell Mr. Audubon he's a fool" (see Scudder's edition of *Keats's Complete Poetical Works and Letters*, 1899). George received numerous letters from his brother John inquiring about life in the wilds of Kentucky (which was far less wild by this point), and in one letter, Keats asks, "Have you shot a Buffalo? Have you met with any Pheasants? My Thoughts are very frequently in a foreign Country—I live more out of England than in it—the Mountains of Tartary are a favourite lounge, if I happen to miss the Allegany ridge, or have no whim for Savoy." In another letter, Keats says, "If I had a prayer to make for any great good...it should be that one of your Children should be the first American Poet" (see Keats's *Letters*, edited by Robert Gittings). Of special interest is the fact that Keats also sent his brother and sister-in-law copies and drafts of certain poems—such as "Fancy," which features the lovely and provocative lines, "Let the winged Fancy roam, / Pleasure never is at home"—prior to their publication. Here's a most remarkable tidbit: on a visit back to England in January of 1820, George copied "Ode to a Nightingale" from Keats's manuscript and "imported" it to Kentucky *before* it was published in England (see Keats's letter to his sister-in-law, Georgiana, January 13, 1820, in Scudder).

Perhaps most intriguing, though, is a series of several stanzas buried deep in Byron's *Don Juan*, (canto 8, stanza 5, 61–65) in which Byron casts "General Boon, backwoodsman of Kentucky" in a strikingly Romantic light:

> Of all men, saving Sylla the man-slayer,
>   Who passes for in life and death most lucky,
> Of the great names which in our faces stare,
>   The General Boon, back-woodsman of Kentucky,
> Was happiest amongst mortals anywhere;
>   For killing nothing but a bear or buck, he
> Enjoyed the lonely, vigorous, harmless days
> Of his old age in wilds of deepest maze.
>
> Crime came not near him—she is not the child
>   Of solitude. Health shrank not from him—for
> Her home is in the rarely trodden wild,
>   Where if men seek her not, and death be more
> Their choice than life, forgive them, as beguiled

By habit to what their own hearts abhor,
In cities caged. The present case in point I
Cite is that Boon lived hunting up to ninety;

And what's still stranger left behind a name
For which men vainly decimate the throng,
Not only famous, but of that *good* fame
Without which glory's but a tavern song—
Simple, serene, the *antipodes* of Shame,
Which Hate nor Envy e'er could tinge with wrong;
An active hermit, even in age the child
Of Nature or the man of Ross run wild.

'Tis true he shrank from men even of his nation;—
When they built up unto his darling trees,
He moved some hundred miles off, for a station
Where there were fewer houses and more ease;
The inconvenience of civilisation
Is, that you never can be pleased or please;
But where he met the individual man,
He showed himself as kind as mortal can.

He was not alone: around him grew
A sylvan tribe of children of the chase,
Whose young, unwakened world was ever new,
Nor sword nor sorrow yet had left a trace
On her unwrinkled brow, nor could you view
A frown on Nature's or on human face:
The free-born forest found and kept them free,
And fresh as is a torrent or a tree.

It is likely that one of Byron's sources for Boone was Imlay's *A Topographical Description.*

Traditionally, scholars have suggested that Romanticism began in England and gradually, through the efforts of illuminati like Emerson and Thoreau, made its way across the Atlantic to influence American philosophy and literature. Is it not possible, though, to suggest that English Romanticism has American roots; that, while Romanticism has been seen as an English concept, it might also be seen—if only briefly—as an American *reality*, lived in an uncouth place like Kentucky, by rough-hewn rustics like Boone? Is not Kentucky the real wild place and is not Daniel Boone the Real McCoy?

FINIS.

ACKNOWLEDGMENTS

I would like to thank the Kentucky Order of Old Regulars for friendship and faith. I would also like to thank Mary Swander whose kindness and precision helped get this project off the ground. John Kulka, of Yale University Press, has been unbelievably generous to me and I am grateful. It has been my pleasure to work with Julie Marshall, David Hough, and André Bernard at Harcourt; I have learned much from their professionalism and have appreciated their patience.

Some of these poems originally appeared in the following journals: *The Black Warrior Review*, *The Greensboro Review*, *The Southern Review*, and *Wind*. I am thankful to the editors and staff of these journals for their support. Some of these poems were also published in a limited edition chapbook, *Osage Orange*, in collaboration with Narcissus Press and SpeakEasy Press, Susan Wyssen and Frank Brannon, proprietors.